Life of a Greatest Generation Survivor

by John A Novobilski
Son of Immigrants

Life of a Greatest Generation Survivor
BY John A. Novobilski
© 2008
All rights reserved

No part of this book may be reproduced, stored in a retrieval system, or transmitted by any means, electronic, mechanical, photocopying, recording, or otherwise, without written permission from the author.

ISBN: 978-1-934051-32-0

www.mysticpublishers.com

Mystic Publishers

Published in the United States of America

To Regina, a dear friend and fine PHS class of '43 classmate.

Semper Fi
John   May 2009

JOHN A. NOVOBILSKI
MANAGEMENT CONSULTANT

8180 CANTO AVENUE
LAS VEGAS, NV. 89147-5613
TEL: 702.248.3520
E-mail: janovski@cox.net

Life of a Greatest Generation Survivor

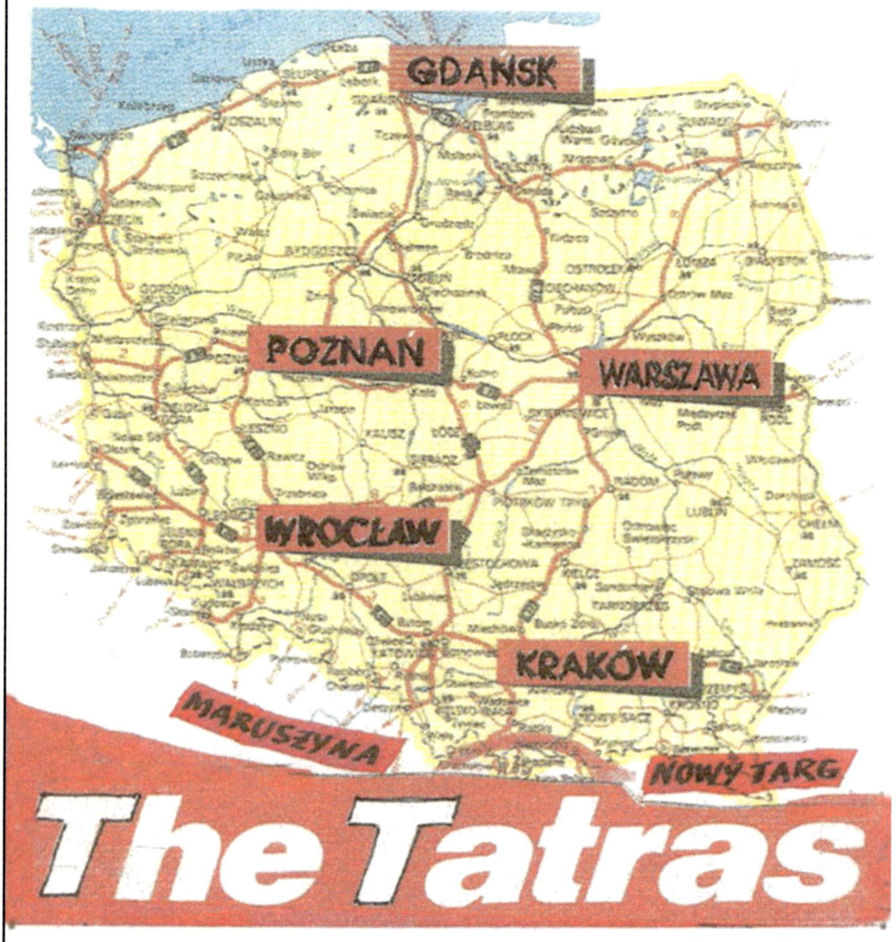

CHICAGO, ILLINOIS

STOWE, PENNSYLVANIA

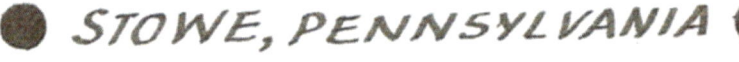

Table of Contents

Foreword...xiii

Parents' Life in Southern Poland...1

Better Life in America - South Side of Chicago?...3

Farmlands Of Pennsylvania...6

Labor Intensive Industries...53

The Great Depression...58

World War II...63

Post World War II...96

College - Beyond Any Kind of Expectation...112

Opportunities in the Power Industry...114

America is Being Destroyed...160

Closing Remarks...188

Note: All documents are located at the end of the book

Life of a Greatest Generation Survivor

by John A. Novobilski
Son of Immigrants

Introduction

This story is based on the memories of the author—son of immigrants—and data gathered from family documents, pictures, and sources noted below. It begins with the history of my parents Anna Skobel and Frank Nowobilski, immigrants from the Podhale region of southern Poland, and covers the life story of the author.

Sources used in this book include:

1. World War II by Polmar and Allen.
2. World War II and Korean Conflict Experience (1995 edition) by the author.
3. Skobel Family Genealogy Chart by Aniela (Skobel) Wrobel and Margaret (Skobel) Gladoch.
4. Book of Podhale Families Geneaology by Maria and Josef Krzeptowscy Jasinek.
5. Official military records of the author.
6. Family picture albums.
7. Information gathered during trips to Poland in 1994 and 2000.

The last chapter explores how America is being destroyed by our 535 politicians refusing to act on important issues, decisions made by our courts, actions of organizations like the ACLU, the secular progressive movement, out of control promiscuity, unnatural and filthy gay lifestyles, epidemic of pedophilia, fatherless out of wedlock children and other social ills, bad environmental laws, and the advancement of the left wing agenda by a biased media and college professors and administration.

Millions of military veterans like me (and millions in the civilian population) who sacrificed greatly to win World War II, never envisioned how our country, the land of freedom, would be destroyed from within.

-- John A. Novobilski
2008

Foreword

With great honor and respect, this story is dedicated to Anna Skobel and Frank Nowobielski (Novobilski) who were born in Southern Poland at the base of the northern border of the Tatra Mountains. This area is generally referred to as the Podhale region. To the south of the Tatra Mountains was the country of Czechoslovakia, which has since been split into the Czech Republic and Slovakia. See DOCUMENT 1, Map of Southern Poland Podhale region. NOTE: All Documents at end of story.

Anna was born in the small town of Maruszyna on a 320-acre farm, which is still owned by the Skobel family. The compound consists of a wood-frame house, a well for fresh water, and a barn for several cows and other livestock. A toilet (outhouse) is adjacent to the house and a barn for hay and animal feed is along side. PICTURES 1, 2 and 3 show some of the buildings of the compound in the background.

The Skobels' livelihood was based on raising animals and planting and harvesting various crops. Milk was a staple obtained by raising one or two milk cows. Anna was the fourth of seven children, five girls and two boys: Agnes (1886-1962), Maria (1889-), Rosalie (1891-), Anna (1893-1975), Aniela (1896-), Wojciech/Adalbert (1899-1969), and Joseph (1903-1993). All of the children were born in the family home. Anna attended a local grade school through the fourth grade. When she was fifteen, she relocated about sixteen miles south to the city of Zakopane to work as a servant at an inn. At age seventeen Anna migrated to Chicago, Illinois.

PICTURES 1, 2 and 3 – *Farm Buildings in background Maruszyna, Poland where Mom - Anna (Skobel) Novobilski was born in 1893. Niece Aniela (Skobel) Wrobel stands in foreground circa 1960. 1-Old Hay Wagon, 2-In front of windows at "White Room" and 3-In front of kitchen windows. Note: Extensive use of wood on buildings.*

My father Frank (1889-1956) was born in Nowy Targ, a town located about twenty miles north of Zakopane. Every Thursday just about everything was traded including: horses, livestock and farm materials, and supplies. His father Franciszek was born in 1844 and he owned many acres of farm and forestland. Frank was the youngest of seven children, four sons and three daughters. Antoinette (1874-) died at an early age of pneumonia, Anna (1878-1946), Wojciech/Adalbert (1879- 1920?), Jan (1881-1919?) was studying to be a doctor and was killed in WWI, Aniela (1883-1953), Frank (1886-1888) died at age two, the second Frank, my father, (1889-1956) migrated to Chicago,

Illinois via Maryland about 1910. The Nowobielski family, as I've been told, is held in high esteem. Many of its members were involved in local government and were considered protectors of the common people. They held the position of mayor and council member in towns and cities. Also, many Novobilski men and boys fought valiantly in the Polish military against invaders.

PICTURES 4 and 5 – *Shows the inside of the "WHITE ROOM" taken in 1993. Religious pictures and special Souvenir pictures shown are presented to each child on their First Holy Communion Day. Yes this is a "special" room where religious commitments are born.*

Parents' Life in Southern Poland

Today the Zakopane region is well known. People from all over Europe travel there to enjoy skiing in the winter and mountain hiking and riding the rapids of local rivers in the summer. Zakopane is a fairly large city with a population of about 30,000 inhabitants. Also, about 2 ½ million tourists visit annually. Snow lies in the Tatra Mountains for 120 to 140 days per year. It is interesting to note that the climate is relatively warm and mild compared to Nowy Targ, which is at a lower elevation. Zakopane is also a cultural center with many quaint places to visit such as the Tatra Museum, the Stanislaw Witkiewicz Museum of the Zakopane Style, the Old Wooden church built in 1848, and traditional homes. On our trips to Zakopane and surrounding area in 1994 and 2000, we walked to some of the same places as Mom and Pop.

A book that my daughter Annemarie (with the help of Margaret Wnuk of Zakopane) discovered about the Nowobilski family told how in the year 1637, King Wladyslaw the Fourth gave to Adalbert (Wojciech) Nowobilski the village of BIALKA. This gift was confirmed in 1938, though the land measurements were given in the old way of measuring land (one lany [field] frankonskie = 23 to 28 Hectares), a method which has not been used for more than 200 years.

John A. Nowobilski

The village BIALKA NOWA included meadows, pastureland, forests, and glades. The 1938 confirmation showed that the Nowobilski family was owners of several sections of named glades and pasturelands: Morskie Oko, Piec Stawow, Woloszyn, Polanica, Lysa, Kiczora, Jaworzyna Wegierska, and Ryniasowka. In addition to all of these were lands that had no names. Taken together, the Nowobilski holdings were among the largest in the area, and they were one of the richest families in the Podhale region! Refer to Map, DOCUMENT 1.

I have been told that Frank, as a youngster, played in the woods during school hours; then he would beat up on his classmates if they did not tell him about the lessons in class. I do not have any record of his schooling in the Nowy Targ area. A tough life at menial labor in Chicago was not his dream, but at least he was able to relocate to a Polish neighborhood on the south side near the stockyards.

It makes me sad that we did not document more about our parents' life in Poland and Chicago. I guess with the language differences (we kids were not schooled in Polish) and our struggles to live our own lives under all sorts of discrimination, we were inundated with as much as we could handle.

Better Life in America?

In those days, there were no fancy colored brochures to entice people to make a long and arduous trip primarily by tramp steamer. Anna Skobel traveled from Zakopane to Antwerp by horse and wagon during the middle of winter suffering through the blustery winds, snow, and extreme cold. The next part of the trip, two weeks aboard ship from Antwerp to New York City, was also tough and uncomfortable. She departed from Antwerp on February 19, 1910 at age seventeen. The whole trip took about a month. Compare this to a flight today, which would take fewer than twenty-four hours! And the US government did not provide any "freebies" as is the case today. These poor folks *did not know the language,* laws, or customs of their new land. Fortunately, they were able to move into an area in Chicago occupied primarily by immigrants from Poland and other Slavic countries. However, most of the available jobs were in shops and factories owned and operated by Americans or immigrants from other countries who were well versed in American ways. This led to a lot of exploitation and unfair treatment.

As I recall, Anna Skobel worked in a glove factory and Frank Novobilski worked in the Chicago Stock Yards – not exactly the greatest place to make a living. No doubt they

John A. Novobilski

had second thoughts about migrating to this hard life from their beautiful pastoral surroundings in southern Poland. The Jungle by Upton Sinclair, describes the unsanitary meat packing industry with its terrible slave-like working conditions and exploitation of workers, especially immigrants hired to work in the stockyards.

Anna's older sister, Agnes (Skobel) Stremp, who had migrated to Chicago several years earlier, owned and operated a boarding house in the Polish area on the south side of Chicago. It was here that Anna lived when she first arrived in America. Meanwhile, Frank migrated to Chicago with his sister Anna (Hovanec, Shervais) who was ten years older and had been to the U.S.A. as early as 1904. At the boarding house, Anna Skobel met Frank, a proud Goral who visited local taverns displaying his strength by lifting the end of a pool table with his teeth.

On May 31, 1913 Anna Skobel and Frank Novobilski were married in a Polish Catholic Church. It was a classic affair with a half dozen bridesmaids and grooms. Gorali musicians played the old familiar tunes from the Podhale region of southern Poland. The favorite drink was the "boiler maker" - a glass of beer and a shot of vodka. There was a lot of dancing and the event went on for a few days! See PICTURE 6, Wedding Day.

As the years went by the family grew – George Walter (1914-1952) named in honor of Frank's relative who also migrated to the U.S.A., Antoinette Marie (1915-2004) named after Frank's sister who died at an early age in Poland, and Anna Mae (1920-1995). All three children were born in Chicago with a midwife handling the births – no hospitals involved. Incidentally, Frank's brother Adalbert died in his early forties, in Pennsylvania. After becoming overheated at work and quickly consuming a very cold drink, he suffered a stroke or heart attack. About 1921 the Novobilski family moved to Pennsylvania to live closer to Frank's sister Anna's family. Pop worked in a coal mine for a short time in Pennsylvania, and I recall seeing his miners cap with a lamp on the front. The cap was stored in the attic of the Stowe house.

Anna Skobel & Frank Novobilski Wedding (3rd & 4th from left front) Chicago, IL (Southside) May 1913

PICTURE 6 – *Wedding Day for Anna Skobel and Frank Novobilski on May 31, 1913 in the south side of Chicago, Illinois. A Polish Priest performed the marriage ceremony in a local Polish church. The affair was carried out according to the Mountaineer (Goral) traditions of the people of the Podhale region of Southern Poland. ~ NA ZDROWIE !*

Farmlands of Pennsylvania

The Novobilski' three youngest children - Levina Aniela (1922-2007), John Albert (1925-) and Angeline Nancy (1932- 1972)- were all born in Stowe, PA. Again, a midwife, usually Aunt Anna, did what was needed. My own birth occurred as follows: Mom, Aunt Anna and cousin Steve were in my aunt's cornfield when Mom told my aunt that she was about to have the baby. They went back to Aunt Anna's house where I was born on August 15, 1925. Coincidentally, my birth date is the same as cousin Steve's, except he was born in 1916.

At this time my parents were making payments on a house built about 1915 by Hungarian immigrants on a hillside lot next to a cemetery. The house price and payments were relatively low, but so were the wages. I cannot imagine what a burden it was to keep up those payments. See PICTURE 7 of the house taken in 1981.

PICTURE 7 – *House on Grosstown Road, Stowe, Pennsylvania, next to the Holy Trinity Cemetery. This photo was taken 1981. Note the rolling hills ahead south toward the original PA. Route 422, which is one mile away.*

The street in front of the house, Grosstown Road, was a gravel street and there were no sidewalks, curbs or gutters. A fall onto the gravel road usually resulted in a wound full of dirt and grit, but a trip to the doctor was not even a consideration. Walking along the street was difficult and dangerous, especially when it rained or snowed. We seldom had protective "rubbers" or galoshes. Across the street from our house was a power pole with a light about twelve feet above ground. During snowstorms, it was exciting to watch the flakes of snow fall against the light, but there was always the worry of how bad it might be in the morning when we walked to school or church. Snow provided lots of challenges. One challenge for a young boy was to "whiz" into the snow writing his name! PICTURE 8, taken in front of the porch in 1929, shows Cousin Dickie, John and sister Levina.

PICTURE 8 - *Grosstown Road house with Cousin "Dickie," John and Levina in front of porch railing taken in 1929 during the "Great Depression." Note: Clothes styles from exclusive Stowe PA. "Rag Bag Shoppe."*

Our house was less than 1000 square feet. The front door and porch faced east. The front porch ran the width of the house and was made of wood. Many times in the summer we slept on the porch to get some relief from the heat and humidity. Though, at any moment we might end up scurrying into the house because someone said that they'd heard a ghost!

The house was a single-story wood-frame building with a partial basement and an unfinished attic. In the basement, anyone above five foot six had to duck to keep from getting knocked out on the floor joists. There was one window down there, about two feet by three, which was used primarily to accept coal and firewood. Once the coal was dumped onto the steel chute and funneled into the cellar, it had to be moved manually to the southwest corner since the stairway was in direct line with the window. The furnace, which burned coal or wood, was located in the northwest corner of the cellar. It provided hot water to the large cast iron radiators in four of the upstairs rooms. The remaining two rooms, the kitchen and the "catch all" room, were not heated in winter. There was a crawl space under this portion of the house where I used to work on my bicycle and carts when it was raining or cold. The kitchen had a stove (it also burned coal or wood) used for warmth, heating water and preparing food. The "catch all" room had an icebox to preserve perishables in the summer.

None of the rooms had any insulation in the walls, ceiling, or attic. To my knowledge, insulation was an unknown building material at that time. The inside walls were plastered onto wooden lath, and those in the unheated part of the house used to end up on the floor from the freezing and thawing process. We did have an electric light in each room but no telephone until 1946. Considering the multitude of phones people have today, it is mind-boggling to think how we got by without even one.

PICTURE 9 - *House on Grosstown Road taken in 1929 the "Great Depression" era. Shows Mom, John, Antoinette and Anna on back steps from catch all room which leads to the hand operated water pump from a deep well. Note: Crawl space under house where John worked on carts and bike during bad weather.*

There were no closets in any of the rooms. We used nails in the walls and piled stuff on chairs or where ever one could find a spot to drop things off. Later, we got a little relief with a kitchen cabinet and a couple of chests of drawers.

Our water supply and toilet were located outside of the house. We used a hand pump to extract water from a 250 ft. well. The cemetery was only about fourteen feet or so from our water well, and I often wondered if the burial of people who were embalmed with various chemicals might lead to contamination of our water supply. In those days there were no federal, state, or local agencies checking any of the water used for consumption – probably just as well without government intrusion. The water was refreshing and cold and satisfying in the warm months. Many people stopped by to ask for a drink. In the winter, it was a hazardous chore climbing down the icy steps to get water for the house with buckets.

Life of a Greatest Generation Survivor

Bathing was also difficult and often postponed. We had to carry in buckets of water and pour it into a large copper or galvanized steel tub, which was heated on top of the stove. It required much attention to keep the fire going and heat the water. Once the water was hot enough, we moved the heavy tub to the floor or set it on a couple of chairs and the children would take turns bathing. It was our dear mother who usually did all of this backbreaking work. Can you imagine a mother in this day and age taking on such a chore?

Mom was a homemaker and her workload with six children was never ending. Just think about it: there were no indoor bath or restroom facilities, cooking a hot meal or heating water required making a fire in the stove, there was no refrigerator, washing machine, or dryer, and no vacuum cleaner. To clean a rug you had to drag it outside, hang it on a clothesline and then whip the hell out of it with a stick or broom handle. What a dusty and dirty job. It usually took at least two people. By the way, there were no summer vacations to the beach or any other place. I can hear the whining of today's lady of the house! Today the protests and bra burning would reach critical mass with all of the lesbian leaders of NOW storming the White House to demand justice.

The toilet (outhouse) was a "two holer" about thirty-five fast paces from the house. Winter use was infrequent because of the cold weather. In summer, the stench was terrible! A Chicago Spiegel catalogue (similar to the Sears catalogue of today) adorned the wall, its slick pages serving as toilet paper.

PICTURE 10 – *Taken in 1939 on Grosstown Road property in front of grape arbor shows Mom, Pop, Aunt Anna (Pop's sister) and Angie. Looks like they just got off the ship at New York Harbor.*

We had an in-house bucket for winter use. These primitive bathing and sanitation facilities quite frankly did not lead to good health habits. Actually, most of the housing in the area lacked good sanitation. These conditions improved in the late 1950's when the town finally installed a sewer system, but our family had moved on by then.

Still, it was a great place for a young man to grow up, with cherry, peach, pear, apple and sour cherry trees and a heavily wooded forest behind the large yard. See PICTURE 10 which shows our grape arbor.

The roof of our house was made of sheet steel and the outside walls were made of painted wood siding. This combination of materials resulted in very hot and stuffy summers and poor heat retention in the winter. Later, we had asphalt-type shingles (with a brick-type look) installed on the outside walls. This improved the house's appearance and cut out the need for periodic scraping and painting. In the summer we kept the windows open and mosquitoes and flies were nuisances. We used a lot of sticky flypaper. The rain barrel that we used to catch water from the rain gutters (the girls used it to wash their hair) was a mosquito breeding pool! When I was in the seventh or eighth grade and had to come up with a project for woodshop, I decided to build wood-frame screens for all of the windows. What a pleasant relief. Everyone in the family really liked the change. That same year, I also built a towel rack. Unfortunately, the metal cross bar rusted and it became impractical!

Back then we kept chickens for their eggs – a staple food in our diet. There were several geese and ducks, too. When I was three or four years old, I remember a gander running after me to take a bite of my backside. Pop caught the gander and heaved it up against a tree, knocking it out cold for a minute – no more action from goosy gander. Cousin Dickie and I would nail a bottomless bushel basket to the top of the chicken coop and play basketball until it got dark. We'd each pick the name of a professional basketball team. We also played baseball across the street from our house - driving the ball over the cemetery fence was a home run. One day I pitched the ball and Dickie hit it right back at me and it hit me in my stomach just below the breastbone. I crumpled to the ground knocked out! After I came to we had a big laugh and back to the game we went. The THRILL of VICTORY and the AGONY of DEFEAT!

Pop used to hire a local farmer to plow about two-thirds of our lot in preparation for planting crops. After the horse-drawn plowing was done, we used to go and break up the large clods and then spread manure and other fertilizers to enhance the poor soil. Next, we used rakes to level the soil and then made furrows to plant seeds, small plants, bulbs or potato halves. We depended on the rain for irrigation. As for pest control, we spent lots of time knocking bugs into cans. Later, we would hammer stakes into the ground to support the tomato plants and string beans. Sweet corn was a favorite of mine. Many times I would strip off a couple ears and eat them raw. Also, field-ripened tomatoes were delicious and nourishing – another one of my favorite foods. At the end of the harvest we would cut and shuck the corn. Dried corn made good chicken feed. The remaining tomato, potato, and bean bushes would dry out and get plowed under next season.

Stowe, Pennsylvania was a small community with a population of 2200. The population now has reached about 3800. It is located about 50 miles northwest of Philadelphia. The town was made up of first and second generation Italian, Hungarian, Slovak, German, Polish, Israeli, Russian, Dutch, Irish, Swedish and British immigrants.

Just to get a flavor of some of the family names look at these: Juhasz, Peto, Plasco, Varady, Testa, Jacketti, Graziano, Bucciaglia, Segneri, Bolonski, Razmyslowski, Breslawski, Zezenski, Waresak, Gofus, Hish, Slaby, Ferenz, Malak, Ludwig, Weaver, Wright, Fritsch, Hauptman, Trout, Knopp, Stauffer, Rubright, Hatlasky, Klaptosky, Phillips, Miklusak, Dazuk, Onufryk, Leary, Pickar, Mace, Norton, Cooney, Wein, Neiman, Estreicher, Faithful, Clark, Mest, Levengood, Brown, Barrett, Maimone, Moyer, Boyer, Yocum, Rauenzahn, Egolf, Surman, Cepohowicz, Capaldi and Kalis. The town was a true melting pot of immigrants who loved their new country.

Like any small town, Stowe had its share of local characters. There was "Crazy Tony" who lived in a shack he built from

Life of a Greatest Generation Survivor

scrap sheets of metal, wood, and cardboard. His "squatters" castle was built among the rusty remains of an old torn down steel mill. At least once a day he would come out of his shack with a large stick and, swearing loudly in Italian, attack the ground or a mound of dirt. This would go on for several minutes. We watched from our hiding places as he took a break for a few minutes then started his tirade all over again. Eventually he would tire himself out and go back to his shack. After dark, he would come out and rummage through trashcans behind diners and restaurants. We never knew what his real problems were or where he came from, and there were no local or state agencies show any concern for the man.

"Pepper Martin" had a "squatters" shack on the same abandoned steel mill land as Crazy Tony, though the men did not mingle. Whatever the weather, Pepper always wore a heavy winter overcoat, with shiny, snot- covered sleeves. During the day, he would write on sheet after sheet of paper then tear the paper into shreds. Like Crazy Tony, Pepper made the rounds for food after it was dark, and the trashcans behind restaurants were his favorites. We kids were scared of both guys, but we always believed that we could out run them. To my knowledge they never hurt anyone.

A younger guy named "Jake" (who was about ten years older than me) was a very athletic and funny person. He seldom held a job and would "bum" a meal or a few cents from the people he hung around with. Jake was an excellent diver. I saw him dive off a bridge ten or twelve feet high into water which was only three or four feet deep. He would "skim" the water about two feet deep and shoot out unhurt. I was never sure of his mental abilities.

A boy who lived up the street from our house in a family of thirteen children aroused my curiosity. "Slick" was about four years older than me and had a business selling bicycles. It turns out he would hitchhike twenty miles to the town of Reading, borrow a bicycle, then pedal it home to place it on sale. He made quite a profit out of this scheme and, to my knowledge, was never caught. I have joked with him about the business. He just grinned with a sheepish look of who me?

Another unusual person in Stowe was a guy named Jack who lived with his wife in a very small house he built close by. The house had about 300 square feet of living space. They had no car or bicycle, and five or six days per week Jack walked the five miles to and from his job at a scrap yard where he operated a large metal shear. What amazed me was that he made the walk in the rain, snow, sleet or hail and, as I recall, he never missed a day of work. He would not spend a dime on the bus. They had several children and they kept living in the small house. He was related to Jake, and I am almost positive that neither of them was operating with a full deck.

There was a guy, about twenty years old, we called "The Hat" since he always wore a chauffer type cap with a short brim and he drove around on a motorcycle. He quit school after the fifth or sixth grade, and many of us would get him fuming by knocking the hat off his head. Most of his hair disappeared due to a disease or for some other reason we did not know. Also, he was very backward. It bothered him terribly when word got around that his sister gave birth to a black child. His sister was never seen outside of the

Life of a Greatest Generation Survivor

Honkey Row apartment where they lived.

A guy we called "Merv" was a skinny, nervous type. I worked with him on a junk truck and with my cart collecting scrap metal. He quit school after the eighth or ninth grade. His primary goal was to work, have money, and own a car to pick up babes. His first car was a 1937 Ford Tudor with a 65 hp engine. You know about Bill Clinton's addiction to women? Well, that is what Merv had. He could be seen almost any time of the day or night, when he was not working, with a gal snuggled next to him as he drove around town. By the way, Merv was one of the best marble shooters. We kids used to play right in the street since auto traffic was not a problem.

"Magyar Bachee" (I think this means Hungarian man) was a man in his fifties who became a "squatter" on a hill belonging to a local farmer. We could see his mess of a place from our house. He built a shack from sheet metal, tarpaper, wood, and cardboard. Bachee collected anything and everything he could find and stored it around his shack. He only spoke Hungarian and our communications with him were generally by hand and facial movements. Most people were concerned about Bachee's prowess as a collector, especially when their own things went missing!

Skeeter the "Midget" was born to a normal family. Well liked by all, he was the center of attention at any gathering because of his size. He always tried to help people and he even joined the West End Volunteer Fire Company in Stowe. He worked at Dana/Spicers in the section where drive shafts were made and retired after over twenty-five years on the job. I used to see him when we went back for the Pottstown High School reunions and visited the Firehouse bar.

If one ever wanted to see a gangster/ mafia type all you had to do was to find the nearest dice game and surely "Sharkey" would be there. He was a slim guy who used to dress in a suit and tie. When his turn came to roll, he would always place one die atop the other and then, with a snap of the wrist, try to spin them to produce his number. In spite of this skill, he actually lost more often than he won. Sharkey was well known for his gambling addiction. He could have been a star in a movie depicting a stereotypical gambler-hustler.

"Eddie" was the town drunk. I met him while working as a "Swamper" on a natural gas pipeline, my job number thirty-three. At the time, he was a recovered alcoholic, and the stories he told me about his drunken adventures were as sad as they were funny. He'd had at least sixteen fights while drunk, and he said he never landed a blow! On one occasion, he was knocked out and lay in the snow for hours. It was only because he was so saturated with alcohol that none of his body parts froze. During his drinking years, Eddie would occasionally work on an ice delivery truck. A favorite bar of his was on the delivery route at the corner of the main drag and a side street. Before the truck reached the corner, Eddie would jump off and scurry through the front door of the bar where the bartender had a double shot of whiskey and a small glass of beer waiting. He would down the drinks and fly out the back door in time to catch the rear end of the ice truck as it turned the corner. Eddie said he hit rock bottom one night while drinking cheap wine in his bedroom. Suddenly the room was crawling with large snakes, elephants, and other outlandish creatures. His screaming landed him in the hospital where he began a recovery program. He had been sober for two years when he was hired to work on the pipeline.

Quite a few families in Stowe lived in "row" houses. Many were white and there were about forty or fifty black families. There was Honkey Row, Lemon Street Row, Colored Row, Hemlock Row, Flaggs Row and others where from eight to twelve two-or-three-stories duplex units were built side by side. Town meetings or social functions were held at the West Pottsgrove Junior High School, the West End Firehouse, St. Gabriel's Italian Hall, or any of the five or six churches of different denominations. We had a volunteer fire company operated by local grocers, barbers, factory workers, farmers, shoemakers and various other craftsmen. Uniforms, boots, and helmets for these volunteers were purchased with monies made from special events. These guys were dedicated to their part-time avocation. Though conditions could be trying, their goal was to knock down fires and help their neighbors in times of dire need.

The Christmas season in Stowe was especially fun. We kids looked forward with joy and happiness to getting a little box of hard candy and an orange – all provided by the volunteer firemen. What a treat! Also, Mom tried to replicate our table to look like it might be back in Maruszyna, Poland. There were lots of different foods like ham, sour kraut, dark bread, mushrooms, red beet horseradish, sausage, honey, pastries and wafers (oplatki). A small piece of the oplatki was passed to everyone at the table along with wishes for good health and prosperity in the coming year. We usually cut our own Christmas tree in the wooded area behind our property. We adorned it with religious and homemade trinkets and placed little gift packages around the base. Mom always had our home blessed before Christmas by a Polish church priest. I still remember seeing K+M+B 19_ _ chalked above the doors: this represented the three Wise Men – Kaspar, Melchior and Balthazar.

Growing up as the son of Polish immigrants, it was difficult to understand the hardships and traumatic times they had to endure. To this day, it makes me feel heartsick to know that I could not appreciate what they went through and that I did not try to understand their problems. Actually, I had enough of my own problems. As you probably know, kids are often very cruel, and a burden I had to carry for years was the fact that my head was larger than normal. The rude comments and ridicule was rough, though eventually my body caught up some. This and careful hair combing disguised the feature. Consider that this pain was on top of the basic discrimination the children of Polish immigrants suffered along with their parents. It would have been easy for a kid like me to take the wrong path in life and become a corruptive youth, a convict, or a free-loading bum!

To avoid discrimination, there were many times I thought of changing my last name to eliminate the "ski". I considered Noble (my nick-name in school), Novo, Nova, Noval, Nobel and Novis. Many people with last names ending in "ski" legally changed their name to try to avoid discrimination. I decided to use my unchanged last name and prove my worth in ways that had nothing to do with the "ski".

I will never know how life would have been if my parents had not made the difficult and frustrating move to the U.S.A. Obviously, with wars, the hardships of communist rule, and food shortages, my life there would have been radically different from the one I ended up with. So, I always try to remember the sacrifice my parents made moving to this great country. Many do not appreciate the great U.S.A. The typical whiners, bitchers, screwballs, ACLU, extreme environmentalists, black radicals, hip hoppers, pedophiles, perverts, left-wing professors and politicians, and gay lifestyle advocates who continually try to destroy this country of freedoms and morally sound traditions should be kicked out for life!

In spite of the trials and tribulations my parents had to endure, occasionally they had Goral parties (like in southern Poland mountain country) with a fiddler, viola player and the singing of traditional old mountain tunes. To loosen up the vocal cords, ample quantities of homemade moonshine (180 proof potato White Lightening) and beer was available. These parties often rolled on until the early morning.

We certainly had our share of traumatic times while living in Stowe. On several occasions our house was tagged with a Sheriff's Sale sign, which meant that all back mortgage payments and taxes were due within thirty days or the house had to be vacated and sold. What a terrible time for us kids, wondering whether we would be living out on the streets. As I recall, somehow the cases were always settled and we were allowed to keep our "ghetto" dwelling, which suddenly felt like a palace! To this day I do not know who helped us keep our home on these sad occasions. We were grateful to them!

Several times Pop was arrested for making and selling moonshine. It so happened that other families were also making and selling moonshine, and Pop supposedly sold his product at a lower price than his competitors. They reported his operations to the local sheriff, and he was subsequently arrested and slammed in jail. You will never know the heartache, anguish, and shame we kids had to face at school, at church, and on the street. People would yell, "You lousy foreign moonshine makers and bootleggers!"

These negative events had a lasting effect on all of our family, making us very shy and introverted. It took me quite a long time to shake this inner conflict - enlisting in the Marines at age eighteen helped. Also, I would tell myself that I was as capable as the next person, and the proof of this would show in my deeds and goals. I took the attitude that no one (not salesman, doctor, lawyer, boss, politician, priest or whoever) was going to intimidate me as long as I had the facts and truth to back up my actions. Another reason for my assertiveness came about due to the court trial of Pop vs. Stanley G. Flagg Co., his employer, concerning an injury Pop suffered while on the job. Prior to the trial, I heard the degrading and derogatory remarks being made against Pop by the defense lawyers for Flagg. Although I was only eleven or twelve, I could hear them say that they would win easily, since Pop supposedly had a country bumpkin lawyer. There were no free, taxpayer-supplied lawyers in those days. Well, those "blue suede shoes" shark lawyers were right. Not only did my father fail to receive any kind of compensation for his injury, he also lost his job. What a blow for our family. The entire incident left me with a deep distrust of people in the legal profession. They are famous for changing the subject to irrelevant issues and using rhetoric that is damaging to the plaintiff, confuses the jury and, in the end, clouds the truth.

After the trial, with what little income that came in from Pop's job no longer available and no savings, our family faced a bleak future. If welfare and food stamp payments had been available then as they are today, I think my parents would have been too proud to sign up for this government assistance. We would have continued to struggle and our poor relatives would have tried to help. About 1936 our dear sister Antoinette, we called her Annette, took a job as a maid for a Jewish family in Pawtucket, Rhode Island. This enabled her to send a few dollars home to help maintain a subsistence level for the rest of us. Pop's sister, Aunt Aniela lived in Rhode Island and she was the one who helped Annette get the job and gave her moral support. It was hard for a young girl to move 250 miles from home, but Annette was a saint who was always willing to help others. When our sister Anna was recovering from mental illness and Mom was getting older, Annette worked at the Spicer (Dana) auto parts factory where she had to handle heavy drive shafts and operate punch presses. It was a demanding job based on piecework, but she did it and used her earnings to help maintain an apartment for herself, Mom, and Anna.

The cellar at the house in Stowe may have been damp and dank, but we used it for many activities. Besides making moonshine, Pop used to make beer. I was, a co-conspirator by collecting bottle caps with which we capped the "new - used" beer bottles. Occasionally, a bottle would explode and make a loud bang like a rifle shot. Someone would holler "call the police" – shucks we have no phone! We also made sour kraut in the cellar by shredding fresh cabbage and packing it into a barrel to be seasoned. Pop would stomp it with his clean bare feet. Then it was covered and allowed to ferment. We also canned vegetables such as corn, string beans, lima beans, and tomatoes in jars for later use in meals and soups.

Another big and dirty job I inherited was cleaning the cellar after the winter activities. The coal and ash dust got into every nook and cranny of the place. All I had to clean it up with was a kitchen broom, a shovel and a bucket for water from the outside pump. Fortunately, there was a drain in the southeast corner that made its way to the gutter. I would sweep the waste over there and wash it down as well I could.

During the summer we had to cut firewood. Pop would buy a truckload of railroad ties and have them dumped in the yard. Some of the hand tools we used for work with wood and for gardening are shown on DOCUMENT 2. There were no electric or battery operated tools available to make the job easier and faster. We used a two-handled saw to cut an eight-foot-long tie into pieces ten to twelve inches long. For smaller jobs we might use a one-man "buck" saw. Anyway, these twelve-inch logs then had to be chopped into even smaller pieces for use in the kitchen stove and cellar furnace. It was a lot of work, but we had to make sure we had our supply in for the winter. I was always, it seemed to me, selected to do this job of sawing wood while my brother, who was eleven years older, sat around sorting his stamp collection. This was not justice, and the resentment that existed between the two of us carried on for many years. Eventually, after WWII, I got sick and tired of my brother's bullying and decided to beat the hell out of him. Fortunately for him, my Mom pleaded with me to stop. I did.

You know, in those days Pop never bought any nails. We would remove crooked, rusty, and bent nails from old pieces of lumber that we found along the road or in a local dump. I had the job of straightening the nails, however, if I used some, Pop would blow a fuse. Therefore, when I built my cart, I had to save some nails for the project. The cart was a great hauling piece of equipment, much better than our wheelbarrow, and I used it for many tasks. Of course, a shiny new red wagon would have been great, but this would not be the real world !

Life was not all work, though. There were many summer events that were extremely exciting and enjoyable. The day school finished for the summer vacation was the most EUPHORIC time for me! It meant that I could get up early and, taking my four-wheeled cart, meet up with a friend to go and collect scrap metal and other recyclable materials to sell to the local scrap dealer. Sometimes we kids would meet at the Manatawny Creek under the Grosstown Road Bridge, which was built in 1880 and rebuilt in 1932. I visited the bridge in 2004 and found it sorely in need of repairs. It was on this concrete bridge that I used to knock myself out trying to adjust the lousy mechanical brakes (hydraulic brakes were not available on Fords) on my 1938 Ford convertible coupe. We would make a dam between piers under the bridge to raise the water level to about three or five feet for swimming. Most of the time we would bring some soap and take a bath. Avoiding the "cow patties" that came floating in our direction became a challenge. We also had to keep alert for snakes. The swim was refreshing and very much appreciated. However, the mile-long walk back home was sweaty and we generally stopped at the Scissio farm to plead for a nice cup of cold well water. They were nice and obliged us kids. On other occasions we would go fishing in the creek for bass and trout. And, if we got really hungry, which seemed to be always, we would make a raid on a local farmer's cornfield. Other times strawberry patches provided our meal. We'd crawl on our stomachs devouring strawberries, leaves and chunks of dirt. Peach and apple orchards were also good targets. There was always a chance that the farmers might catch us, but we would run at full speed, and all we could hear was a verbal blast of choice words-in English or other languages-ringing in our ears.

The Schuylkill River, which was about two miles from our house, carried water away from the coal mining area. It was full of coal dust and particles because the mines used to wash the coal before delivery. Once my cousin Dickie and I (I was about ten or eleven at the time) went swimming in it. The current was fast compared to the Manatawny Creek. Well, before I swam a few strokes it started to take me downstream faster than I could paddle. Dickie screams at me "just ride the current and guide your body toward the shore and grab on to a branch or root." I finally ended about a quarter of a mile down stream. The whole thing scared the hell out of me. When Dickie and I met on shore, we were pretty black from the dirty water and the coal particles glistened from the sun's rays. That was the last time I ever swam in that river. Now, in 2007, the river has been cleaned up and all types of activities take place on this waterway.

Another activity I enjoyed as a kid was watching the Federal WPA (Works Projects Administration) workers laying concrete for the local part of Pennsylvania Route 422, which was about a mile from our house. WPA was a federal program initiated during the Great Depression by Executive Order to provide jobs to millions of unemployed men and women. Unemployment was high then – about twenty-five percent. There were times when the workers would share something out of their lunch bucket with me, and I was very grateful for their generosity. I spent many days watching concrete being trucked in and dumped between the forms where a mechanically driven screed leveled it to a flat surface. Workers under the WPA did hundreds of different types of jobs from art to construction to engineering, forestry, farming and repairing infrastructure.

Another pastime was to watch gravediggers prepare a hole for a burial. It so happened that the gravedigger team also had a hog farm, and when they arrived at the cemetery they had a load of "old pies" from the nationally famous Smiths' pie bakery. They allowed us to rummage through the pies to see if we were able to get some edible pieces by knocking off the mold or bad spots. We could eat as much as our stomachs could hold – living high on the hog. To supplement our income and find bits of good food we also used to dig in the dump that later became the huge West Pottsgrove Landfill.

Besides swimming and fishing, our summers were filled with pick-up baseball games, races, high jump and broad jump action. We liked the competition and the satisfaction of winning. We certainly kept busy with these wholesome activities. Today's computer games and bookworm events can't compare with our way to spend summer. Active games and events were the order of the day. Along with our limited food intake, the exercise kept us skinny. Obesity did not have a chance to take over our bodies.

Polish picnics were a lot of fun. They often had a band which played Polkas and modern day music for dancing on a wooden floor built by committee members of the church or lodge sponsoring the picnic. We kids usually played games and ran wildly around the place in a wooded area away from traffic. The event usually started about noon and ended at dark. By then the kids were burned out and the adults were tired from dancing and woozy from too much beer.

There were many times that we would go out into the fields to pick wild blackberries and raspberries. Our intention was to get a nice big bucketful and then sell them to the neighbors, but it never worked out that way. We would always eat all of the berries and get home with an empty bucket. My Mom got a big chuckle out of our mission.

You should have seen me when I caught my first fish, a Sun Fish, from a pond close to the Manatawny Creek. The fish was about four inches long and as soon as I landed it the race was on to get home over a mile away. When I got home Mom quickly fried it in butter, but when I went to eat it all I could chomp into were bones! That was a disappointment that put a damper on going fishing for a long time.

The fall season was my favorite time of the year with the beautiful colors of orange, yellow, crimson, brown and gold on the numerous trees that covered the land from our back yard to the wooded area miles beyond. We used to pick walnuts, persimmons, berries and mushrooms that grew wild. Shelling walnuts left our hands stained and dirty looking. It took days for the stains to disappear. Fall season also brought Halloween and a few activities I am not so proud of. Sometimes we would look for an occupied outhouse and tip it over backwards. The occupant would scream some nasty words and we would run and hide and laugh like we were nuts. Another bad prank was to throw rocks at empty milk bottles on a porch and listen to the crash of breaking glass. Afterward, we would run like hell!

Life of a Greatest Generation Survivor

Another bad act that I am not proud of was throwing stones at birds sitting on power lines. Once, when I tossed a stone at a couple of birds on the wires, I hit a little sparrow that soared down at me in what looked like an attack mode. Actually, my stone had hit the bird in one eye and killed the poor thing. I buried the little bird. After that, my attacks on birds sitting on power lines were over!

It always got cold starting in November and stayed cold until about March. Our clothes were definitely not adequate to keep one warm and dry, but it was a great time to play outside sliding down the snow-covered hills on an old car fender. The 1932 and 1933 Ford or Chevy fenders were the best – they would spin around and you would never be able to guide them to your intended destination. One evening, while sledding with a fender, I ended up in a creek that was not completely frozen over. Well, one half of my body got wet. By the time I got home half of my body was frozen. To add to my misery, Pop took the strap to my backside. What a ride. Another stupid stunt was to jump on a sled and grab a car's rear bumper to get a free ride while breathing exhaust gases. One would usually disengage when the car hit a big rut of ice, water, and snow and end up in the soup—a real mess.

We used to ice skate with skates that were attached to our shoes by built-in clamps. However, my shoes were so beat up that the skate clamps would come loose. Also, my ankles were not too cooperative and I would end up in a heap on the ice. My days of trying to become a "class" skater came to an end rather quickly.

John A. Novobilski

Many people these days just love to ski. My sons Carl, Steve, and Frank are very good skiers. They are also excellent surfers. My days skiing were short lived. Back then we only had "barrel staves" for skis. If you can imagine a barrel stave, which is about three feet long and without any full curvature on the end, then you can visualize the problems we had. The staves were attached to your foot by straps nailed to their sides. As you slid along, the front tip of the staves would catch in the snow and you would go head over heels. I did not need a degree in science to understand how many bones I could break. Just thinking about the possible results brought my skiing days to an abrupt halt.

Also, during the winter I would go with my dear cousin Dickie (Aloysius Richard) who was about four years older and my mentor, and set traps to catch muskrats, weasels, skunks, possums, raccoons, and hopefully foxes. The traps were set in the evening. Before school the next day, we would check the traps to harvest our catch. We would later skin the animals and stretch the hides to dry out to sell for between twenty-five and seventy-five cents. There was a time when the Pennsylvania Fish and Game Department would pay us a fifty-cent bounty for weasel hides. A weasel could devastate a chicken farm in one night. A fox fur was much more valuable, but we never caught one. We had some weird experiences trapping: on one occasion I caught a possum and took it to Hemlock Row and there was such a fuss by the black folks as to who wanted the possum the most. I sold it for fifty cents. As you probably know, the possum is a slow and lumbering animal with lots of fat; I never understood why anyone would like the meat loaded with fat. On another occasion my trap had only a muskrat paw. The animal had chewed its leg off to escape. That day at school I was talking to a friend who set traps downstream from mine, and he told me that one of his traps had yielded a muskrat without a paw!

One night Dickie and I walked about three miles from home to a large pond behind a working farm. To our delight we found a string of traps there. We grabbed about twenty-five of them and headed home with the loot. Well, the next night we dummies decided to go back and get some more free traps! Imagine my surprise when a farmer/trapper stuck a gun in my ribs (I almost loaded my trousers) and shouted HALT! He put us in handcuffs and marched us to his house where a Sheriff was waiting to arrest us and take us to our homes to recover the stolen traps. Dickie and I both got our backsides whipped with the old razor strap. Man, did it hurt.

Another incident that is fresh in my memory was the time I caught a skunk in one of my traps. I had to get close to retrieve the critter. This was a hell of a problem because the skunk had only one front leg caught in the trap, leaving the rest of it free to move around. Also, there was a fence on two sides of the skunk. It was cornered. As I tried to get to the skunk to knock it out, it whipped around and blasted me full in the face. Now I stunk like a skunk. I finally got the skunk for skinning, but when I got home all hell broke loose. Since I only had one good shirt and pants, I had to take everything off and hang the pieces on the clothes line in mid-winter. I did not go to school all week and my butt was sore. Those damn skunks were not my favorite animal to trap.

Whatever the weather - rain, sleet, snow, wind, hail - it was the job of me or sister Levina to walk about a third of a mile to pick up our daily supply of fresh milk. There was no homogenizing or pasteurization since it came straight from our neighbor's cow. I do not recall the price. We also had to walk (a little more than a mile) to pick up the mail at the Stowe post office. I still remember we had P. O. Box 47!

A special chore was to take the cart I'd built and travel about a mile away to collect a prickly, milky weed (Pop called it mlatz) for our geese, which ate the stuff with great delight. I also used my cart for collecting scrap metal, rags, hardstock, cardboard and recyclables. Originally, the cart had a steering wheel and a seat with a backrest. A funny thing happened with the steering. My first attempt at making the steering operable resulted in a big error. When I turned the steering wheel to the right, the cart would go left and vice versa. I would let other kids ride it down a hill where they had to turn at the bottom. I used to laugh my head off at the results. Later, I fixed the steering to work properly and eventually converted it to a pull cart. My cart was our way of making a few cents to buy a Royal Crown or Pepsi cola, a sweet pastry, or two or three cigarettes at a penny each. DOCUMENT 3 shows a sketch of both the original and final versions of the cart.

By the way, when I was thirteen or so, a local bicycle shop owner had enough faith and trust in me to sell me a brand new bicycle on weekly payments – no co-signers required. Boy was I some proud kid with a new black and white Rollfast bike. The money to pay for it came from picking up junk, hauling out trash and ashes for local people. It was a bit embarrassing for us to see their own lazy kids at school or on the street. My friends and I were always looking for a job to make a few cents!

Even though we had to work, we still knew how to have fun. We enjoyed all sorts of sports. The sense of achievement and competition was very satisfying. Bowling was popular, but it was costly. However, working as a pin setter at the West End Firehouse was a good way to earn money and learn how to bowl. My brother was a member of the firehouse, so I used to bug the hell out him to get me a pin setter job. To show how determined I was to get the job I spent numerous evenings in a window well where I could see and talk to the guys setting up pins. They would let the alley manger (named "Waxy") know of my presence. Finally, after about a year of persistence, I got the job with my buddies – Don, Steve, Bob and Doug. We were only fifteen or sixteen and, wow, did my school grades suffer. We worked every night from about 6:30 PM to 10:00 PM. On Saturday nights, the regular bowlers would bring their wives to spend an evening bowling, dancing, playing the slot machines (backbone of income) and chatting. Usually, the bowlers would buy a paper plate full of chunks of cheddar cheese, sausage, dill pickles and some pretzels for us pin setters. The food would vaporize with our voracious appetites! One couple that came in on Saturdays was "Cappy" Lau and his wife. Their daughter was in our Pottstown High School class and I still see her at our Class of '43 reunions. Although she was cute, I did not have a chance to date her because boys from Stowe were not favorites of Pottstown girls. Stowe girls did not like us any better. They wanted to date guys from other towns – Stowe guys were terrible. At age fifteen the other pin boys and I joined the local YMCA league. We bowled against about eleven other teams. My brother was on an opposing team. Well, in a match against his team, I bowled a first-prize-winning league high three-game series of 646 with a 245 game, even though my average was 152. He really took a razzing from almost everyone in the league.

PICTURE 11 shows our West Pottsgrove Jr. High School Class of 1941. There were 46 members, 19 girls and 27 boys.

PICTURE 11 - *West Pottsgrove Jr. High School, Stowe, PA. Class of 1941 – in front of school - June 1941.*

And now let me tell the story about our West Pottsgrove Jr. High School football and basketball team records. In the 1940-41 football season we played five games and our record shows: Wins - 0, Losses - 1, and Ties - 4. It was noteworthy that our offense scored zero points. The local Pottstown Mercury, sportswriter Paul Lucas, with whom I became friendly later, wrote a story about our lack of offense and praised our defense which allowed only eighteen points in one game. Our coach told Paul that because we had so few players, most of us played both offense and defense. Also, with so few players it was not possible to have full scrimmages to really test the capabilities of the offense. Our practice field was about two and a half miles from the school and we walked or trotted to the Old Mill Park field and racetrack. Proper equipment was non-existent. We looked like a "rag tag gang" with trousers with little or no padding, helmets so flimsy they could be folded, shoes a couple sizes too large, so that we had to stuff the toes with paper. Our shoulder pads were ragged and the connecting straps were broken or missing.

In spite of the lack of equipment, we still enjoyed the organized mayhem of football, and the players and community had a sense of pride as we represented the Stowe school. DOCUMENT 4 is our won-loss record. DOCUMENT 5 is my Award Letter. One of the most physical of all our games was against Boyertown. This was a team of farmers' sons. Most of these guys weighed fifteen to twenty-five pounds more than we did. Wow, were we exhausted after this game, but we fought them to a tie.

Our basketball team was very competitive and we almost won the MONTCO (Montgomery County) league championship. We practiced at the YWCA in Pottstown, which was over three miles from our school. Getting there was our responsibility – no busing. Our coach used to drive slowly along the route we walked to school. One morning a couple of us were smoking. The coach did not condone this habit and it could lead to being kicked off the team. We had to hide the burning cigarette in our cupped hand, and hide the hand in our trousers. Man oh, man, it took forever for him to get out of our view. We made it, though, and were more careful in the future.

John A. Novobilski

During practices our basketball team had an ample number of players to make the scrimmages more like a real game compared to that of the football team. I played point guard – the person who was responsible for starting the plays that the coach signaled. This was a big responsibility for me, but it made the game much more exciting. We played a non-league game against Warwick High and did we get clobbered. They beat us 53 to 15. Seems that they had several Painter boys, one or two on the team every year, who were very good basketball players and their school's court was a great advantage to them. The court had a surface that was half wood and half asphalt concrete. Also, long shots had to go between the ceiling rafters. We had never seen anything like it and by the time we figured out how to play on it the game was over. DOCUMENT 6 is the record of our basketball team and DOCUMENT 7 is my Award Letter.

By the way, being a member of a sports team made your chances of "getting" a girl much better than if you were just a smart honor roll "dork." Some of my girlfriends were cheerleaders such as Rosie, Marguerite, Martha, and Ruth. Even in those years, "jocks" got some extra benefits for their efforts on the field or court. Even so, dating was limited because nobody had a car and money did not come easily.

The school burned to the ground the year after we graduated. It was a sad sight to see as we lost about twenty-five years of records, class and team pictures, awards and other memorabilia.

My experience in the working world started at an early age – about ten or eleven. I had a lot of different jobs because I was so curious about different industries. Almost all of the

Life of a Greatest Generation Survivor

time I would arrange for a new job before quitting the one I had. Looking at the list of jobs I've had might make one ask why he can't hold a job. However, I really enjoyed the changes and new challenges. I had no trouble finding and keeping jobs because I was always on time (except for one notable exception you will read about later), clean cut, and neatly dressed. Also I stuck to the following principles on the jobs:

1) Ask questions such as:
    a) Why is this operation or process done?
    b) Where is this piece or part used?
    c) How can the job be done better and faster?
    d) When is a part of the job done best?
    e) Where can improvements be made in doing this job?
2) Learn all you can about jobs related to yours.
3) Don't goof off. It is harder to waste time than to keep busy.
4) Work safely. Be alert to unsafe areas of your surroundings.

The following is a brief description of the 33+ jobs I had before I started working in the engineering field:

1) *Junk collector* and helper on a junk truck. In the days before the environmental rage and before the word "recycle" was known, we were busy collecting aluminum, steel, cast iron, brass, copper, rags, and cardboard to sell to scrap dealers, who in turn sold the stuff to processors for recycling.

2) *Trash hauler.* We would canvass local families to

determine if they needed someone to remove the trash and stove/furnace ashes to a dump for a nominal fee. Usually it was embarrassing to them because many of the families had children who were in the same grade in school as we were. It seemed strange that these rich, spoiled, lazy brats could not do the job for their parents! Generally, the dumping spot was close by since there were no official dumps. Trash pickup by large companies was non-existent. Many years passed before West Pottsgrove Township (also referred to as the Pottstown Landfill) became a dumping ground for New York, New Jersey, and other states. This "smelly" arrangement, the result of underhanded political deals, really affected the surrounding community. In an attempt to appease the families living close to the landfill, the waste management company agreed to pay the real estate taxes for all property owners during the life of the dump. The trash pile eventually reached about three hundred feet high, and still the company wanted a contract to go higher and wider. The landfill was finally closed in 2006.

3) *Scrap iron digger.* A steel fabrication plant was abandoned (this was the area where "Crazy Tony" and "Pepper Martin" built their shacks) and the bulk of the main structure salvaged. In this "rust belt" area of about a hundred acres, most of the substructure remained. When I was thirteen, a couple of us kids worked with a very pleasant and ruggedly built black man named Big John digging for scrap iron. Some of the scrap came in plates four to five feet square and ¼" to ½" thick. Big John would help us lift the plates and stack them for the scrap dealer. This was

dirty, backbreaking work. One day I made a "big hit" when my digging led to a pit where rivet hole punchings would drop. Digging out these punchings, which were about one inch in diameter and ¾" thick, gave us a steady job and a good source of scrap iron, though the sharp edges cut up my hands. At the end of the day, a scrap dealer would come and buy our scrap iron. We helped load his truck.

4) *Potato picker.* My Aunt Anna, a mid-wife and Pop's older sister, would feed her son Dickie and me large bowls of vegetable soup until we were filled up to our ears. Then she would walk with us to a local farm to pick potatoes. After a few hours and a few bags of potatoes we were bushed, but she was still going strong. We did this job a few times, but the earnings of a few cents and some potatoes were not encouraging.

5) *Corn shucker.* A local farmer hired a couple of us kids to harvest corn, cut it and shuck it. He would pay us by the number of rows. Talk about a nasty job. We got dirty, sweaty, and scratched up from the sharp edges of corn leaves. The pay was a pittance, but the farmer was ever grateful for the help.

6) *Cesspool digger.* A family that lived close to my Aunt Anna needed help digging a cesspool about twelve feet deep and six feet in diameter. This amounts to about 41,000 lbs., 350 cubic feet, or 1000 buckets of soil. This soil was semi-clay with rocky sections. One of us would dig and fill a bucket with soil and the other one would hoist the bucket up and dump the soil into a low part of the property owner's yard. It was no wonder we were

skin and bones, trying to do men's work without sufficient nourishment. As we dug deeper the chore became more difficult and exhausting. The job was completed in a few days and the pay was lousy.

7) *Wheat Thrasher helper.* This had to be the dirtiest job thus far. In the hottest summer days (with dirt, dust and wheat slivers piercing my face, neck, arms and legs) a day of this work was all I could endure for fifty cents, and I think we got a sandwich, too. One tried to keep the dirt, dust and chafe out of the nose with a wet handkerchief tied across the nose and mouth. Where was OSHA to penalize the farmer for such unhealthy practices? Wow. I developed a rash, which itched like none ever before. Getting clean was an impossible chore. I swore that there would be no more wheat thrashing jobs for me regardless of the pay!

8) *Fur trapper.* Setting traps after school and checking for catches early the next morning was exciting, though it would probably not please "tree huggers" and PETA (People for Ethical Treatment of Animals) in this day and age. The goal was to sell the hides for money to help one to survive. In the case of weasels there was a bounty for each hide paid by the State Fish and Game Department.

9) *Bowling Pin setter.* At the West End Firehouse there were four bowling lanes, and at that time the pins were set up manually. Each wood or plastic pin, about fifteen inches tall with a coke bottle shape, had a hole in its bottom about a half of an inch in diameter and two inches deep. After retrieving the bowler's ball and

placing it on the return track, it was time to set the pins for the next frame. To set the pins, the pin boy would press a pedal under the lane, which would make ten steel spikes protrude above the lane in a triangular pattern. The pin boy would place the pins on these spikes and then release the pedal to disengage them. The pins were then ready for the bowler to continue with the game. We earned four and a half cents per game or, for one match per night with two five-man teams bowling three games, a whopping twenty-two cents per hour.

10) *Bagger/Stocker* at grocery store. At age fifteen I worked at the Acme Market and the A & P market. Both of them were on High Street - the main drag in Pottstown. I would bag the customer's purchased items and at times carry the bags to their car. I got an occasional tip, but not too often. At the A&P my job was to cut, weigh, wrap, and price various cuts of cheese in the dairy section. This was an interesting place to work because the manager wanted me to gain experience in various departments of the store to learn to be a manager. This was somewhat ironic, since he had a son about my age, and the son did not work at the store in any capacity. As it turned out, my military duty interfered with any future in the grocery business. However, it was enjoyable and steady work with good opportunities for advancement. Stocking the shelves required marking or stamping a price on each item and making sure that the newly stocked items were the same price as the existing items. If not, the old items had to be marked with the new price. This was usually backbreaking work.

11) *Visual Casting Inspector.* During World War II many men eighteen years and older were enlisting or being drafted into the services. Under a new law, seventeen-year-old boys and girls were permitted to work in industries manufacturing items to be used in the war effort. This law enabled me to gain employment at the Doehler Die Casting Company. Aluminum castings made on injection die casting machines would be placed on a continuously moving conveyor. These castings moved past a line of steel tables where an inspector removed them from the conveyor and performed a visual inspection. After inspection, the castings were either passed as okay or sent to a rejection pile to be melted down and the metal was used again. I was still a senior at Pottstown High School when I had this job. I would attend classes from 8:30 am to 12:30 pm and then kill time until start of work at 3:00pm. I did not finish work until 11:00pm. Gosh darn it, thanks to the lack sleep my school grades dropped like a rock. Often I had to do some cheating to turn in homework. The job paid sixty cents per hour or twenty-four dollars per week. Most people today can make twenty-four dollars in an hour. At the time though, the pay was enticing and it gave me a lot of freedom, but I did miss almost all extra curricular activities at school, even my graduation ceremony.

12) *Precision Casting Inspector.* A crew of three precision inspectors selected me to work at a higher level of inspection using blueprints and various gages to check the final castings to see that they met government specifications. It was a clean and satisfying job

working with instruments and prints, and it required concentration and focus to verify the results. This job was not monotonous and it was a big advancement for such a young man.

13) *Handyman* at a furniture store. Here was a real flunky job. I had to move, stage, clean and polish furniture in a three-story furniture store owned and operated by Ben "Lumbago" Goldberg. The poor guy had severe arthritis and used to hobble around like someone just booted him in the butt. Harold, the manager of a paint and wallpaper store adjacent to the furniture store, was a fun and friendly guy with lots of jokes. He sure played one on me. He told Ben that he wanted to treat both of us to a hot dog and soda pop. Of course we agreed. You should have heard the laughter when I bit into a rubber hot dog! The damn thing was tough as a tire, but it looked real. The laughter went on for days and I laughed along with Ben and Harold.

14) *Furniture mover.* This was pure labor, but applying the techniques of making moves with leverage principles made it much easier. One move stands out. It was for an elderly couple. The stench of cat and dog crap and urine permeated their house. I almost tossed my breakfast when I walked in. Fortunately, I made it to the street. Then, when we went to move the stove, it slipped out of our hands because it was covered in grease and whatever may have dropped on the edges. That was it for me. We did make the move as we promised, but it was not long before I said goodbye to the furniture moving business.

15) *Machine Shop Apprentice.* This was an easy way for a business owner to get cheap labor since under this program the G.I. Bill would pay half of the apprentice's wages. We worked ten hours Monday through Friday and five hours on Saturday building rock crushing machines which consisted of large body castings with sixteen-inch shafts on opposite ends. Each shaft had hammers to crush rocks up to one foot in diameter. The shafts were mounted on large bearing surfaces. My job was finishing the bearing and mating surfaces manually with scrapers. Between the lousy machinist training and low wages, I quit after a couple weeks.

16) *Plastic Thread machine operator.* This job consisted of operating a machine that extruded heated plastic (PVC) powder into strands of plastic thread. As the six strands of thread ejected we would wind each one onto a reel synchronized to move at the speed of the extrusion. When the reels were full, we had to break the threads, and start up another set and then remove the full reels, All this had to be done while keeping up with the machine. My boss John liked my work and the way I coordinated effort to reduce scrap. One Saturday, working the graveyard shift at double pay, I promised John that he could depend on me to be there since production was behind. Well, it did not work out that way. After working the previous night, a couple of friends and I had spent almost all day bowling and drinking. I only slept a couple of hours. Mom had a terrible time trying to wake me from my "coma." So, off to work I went in a stupor. I could barely stand up and my coordination was so bad that he had to work my machine. Never again did I pull such a stupid and shameful stunt.

Life of a Greatest Generation Survivor

For a long time afterward my boss John would see me and laugh till his jaws hurt.

17) *Tire builder* for truck and passenger cars. Within six months the plastics division had to cut back because of fewer and fewer orders. I was asked to become a truck tire builder. The plastics and tire work was at the Pottstown, Pennsylvania plant. As I recall, the pay was good at about a dollar per hour. I always reached my production goals. Soon they wanted me to become a line leader, responsible for keeping a line of twenty to twenty-five tire builders working at maximum efficiency by attending to such matters as machine repair, stock availability, scrap reduction and tool replacement. My goal was to attend college and I did not think it was possible to do that locally because my friends would coax me to go out drinking and dancing every weekend. I decided to live with my sister and brother-in-law in California and work toward a degree in Mechanical Engineering.

18) *Molder* at a cast iron foundry. I lasted three days on this job. The wages were based on production, and pounding sand into molds and standing by molten iron being poured into the molds was rough. The dirt, dust, smoke, and heat made an eight-hour shift seem like a lifetime. I was miserable. I think I submitted my notice to quit on the second day! Naturally, the old-timers thought my move was reasonable, but it was sad to see that they were stuck in a dead end job.

19) *Peach skins removal* at a pie bakery. This was another three- day job. It was at the nationally famous

Mrs. Smith's frozen pie bakery. A trough-like container about twelve feet long held about twenty bushels of peaches immersed in hot water. My job was to move the peaches around and remove the skins to prepare the fruit for pit removal and cooking to make pies. Not an exciting future.

20) *Oven Tender/ Feeder* at a bread bakery. It was the middle of summer in Pennsylvania – 85 to 95 °F and 80 to 90 % humidity. Feeding the hot oven with rye bread dough would have drained the energy out of anyone. We had a bucket of water with oatmeal mixed in keep us from fainting. This type of work was definitely not in my future!

21) *Degreaser* of aluminum sunglass frames. This was at a little shop that made sunglass frames. My job was to remove the grease and dirt from the frames after they had been buffed to create a shiny surface. I would place several dozen frames in a metal basket and dip them into a vat of TCE (trichloroethylene - where were the environmentalists and OSHA?). Let me tell you, this was a hell of a way to get drunk and stupid fast. I was the wrong guy for this job. A week on this job was too long.

22) *Potato chip maker.* This was a part time job that I took to make some extra bucks. It was kind of a one or two man operation. The owner would help when he came back from his route deliveries. The first step was to dump potatoes into a machine that washed and removed the skins. Once peeled, they went into a slicing machine, which was then adjusted for thickness of

the chips. After a bit of drying, the slices were dumped into a large pot of boiling oil. When the chips became tan colored, we would fish them out with a metal basket strainer, spread them on a drying rack, and apply a generous quantity of salt. Finally the chips went into bags (there were two sizes), which were sealed and placed into boxes for delivery. After an hour of this work one smelled like hot grease.

23) *Pretzel Bender.* Nowadays pretzels are made with machines that produce more pretzels in an hour than one employee could make in a month. Back then, though, I would take an eight-inch length of dough and, grabbing each end, fold the ends over to make a pretzel. Wow, was this a boring operation. This job lasted only a couple of days. The pretzel industry has only survived because of the high production machines. It would have died under the manual process. People in Pennsylvania love their pretzels especially when sitting at a bar sipping beer.

24) *Groundskeeper* at the American Society of Cinematographers club facility in Hollywood. My sister and brother-in-law were employed as caretakers of this building and the associated parking lot and landscaped area. As partial payment for living in the cellar, I helped them maintain the grounds. By then I was attending college with assistance from the G.I. Bill.

25) *Dishwasher* for a kitchenware salesman. My brother-in-law Bernie was working for Guardian Service selling cast aluminum kitchen pots, pans, and other utensils. The sales method was to cook a meal for potential

customers using the products. Each dinner party would have as many as fifteen or twenty guests. Obviously, sale of the pots and pans were of prime importance. As you might imagine, there were always plenty of folks eager to eat the dinner, but when it came to purchases – see you later. This venture was not very successful, especially considering the cost of food and transportation. My job was to clean the dishes, silverware, and pots. A funny thing happened at one house. Bernie placed a hot pot on the windowsill. When I tried to remove it for cleaning it was stuck. I gave it a quick jolt and up came the pot with about ten coats of paint! All I could do was lay on the floor and laugh. Bernie heard me and rushed in to find out what was going on. He sheepishly pointed out the damaged windowsill to the lady of the house, who promptly dismissed it as no problem. We were happy to know we did not have to make any repairs.

26) *Press Operator* of musical recordings. This was another "hum drum" job. It consisted of taking soft bakelite-like material and placing it on the press and moving the top half down to make a record. This was the mother of all boredom.

27) *Survey crew grunt.* A survey crew is composed of an instrument man (crew chief), a tape man, and the grunt pounding the stakes wherever the chief tells him to. When we worked on a busy thoroughfare, crazy and impatient drivers would often try to scare or hit us. One day some jerk swerved at us, and our crew chief threw a rather heavy plumb bob through his rear window – what a crash. The jerk stepped on the gas. He knew better than to stop and argue his case.

Life of a Greatest Generation Survivor

28 & 29) *Post Office sorter and Postal Delivery Man.* These were two jobs that I worked to make some money during the Christmas season. This could be an eye opening experience at times. One met lots of nice and weird people on the delivery rounds.

30) *Janitor.* This was at the Thrifty Drug Stores ice cream plant. What a great job – wallowing in ice cream. I answered an ad for a janitor. The applicant had to be married. Even though I was not married I applied for the job. I convinced the manager that my reliability and work ethic would be as good as (or perhaps even better than) that of a married man because I needed the money while attending college. The job entailed general cleaning, including cleaning toilets and hosing down large amounts of ice cream into a drain. The benefits were great. I got to take home a couple of cartons of ice cream every day. Fortunately, I was very active and the fat from the ice cream did not pile up on my body.

31) *Machine Operator* for a sprinkler manufacturer. It might surprise some to know that a manufacturing plant could be located in Beverly Hills, California. Nevertheless, located on the edge of this city was a small foundry and machine shop where brass and pot-metal sprinkler heads were cast and machined. Brother-in-law Bernie and I worked as operators of lathes and pot-metal casting machines. The sprinkler heads were sold under different brand names. A few years later the city outlawed such operations and the factory was demolished. Since that time, plastic sprinklers have

become the norm because they cost less to manufacture and use. Brass sprinkler heads are available, but they cost more and require more labor to install.

32) *Warehouse worker* at a department store. This was another of my part-time jobs. I retrieved specific products from the warehouse for the woman in charge of the ladies cosmetics counters. The manager was a cute gal with a southern accent who kept me jumping, especially during the busy Christmas holiday season.

33) *Swamper* on a pipeline construction. One summer, when I went back to Pennsylvania in between school semesters, I quit my job at the local bakery (Job 20) to work on the installation of a natural gas pipeline. The pipeline emanated from Texas and it had now reached our area. Some of the employees were "good ole boys" from Texas and Oklahoma, but people were being hired locally to replace those workers who did not follow the job. I was assigned to a crew that lowered a bitumastic-covered pipe into a trench four to five feet deep. Well, the boom operator had a new 1946 Ford convertible coupe and he used to pick up his helper and take him to work daily. After a few weeks, the helper not only had the car, he was also courting the wife of the boom operator! By the way, word around town was that work on the pipeline was hard and dirty. This was false. It was outside work and not nearly as bad as my job at the bakery. It also paid well. We had a lot of "goof off" time, and the foreman appreciated our good work.

34) *Welder helper* for pipeline construction. To get me to continue working on the pipeline as it moved out of

our area, I was offered a better paying and easier job as a welder's helper. The welder I worked with was a slick dude. We would spend most of the day riding up and down the project. Then, around quitting time, we would track down the big boss and let him know we were behind schedule and would require overtime. Soon, though, it was time for me to get ready for the next school semester so I had to quit the pipeline construction work. This was a truly fine experience.

35) *Time Study Analyst* at the Aluminum Company of America (ALCOA). When I got this job studying and timing the various aluminum Ingot Plant operations, I was also working as a tire builder at Firestone. I only lasted a couple of weeks as a time study analyst because my boss came to me after about four days and said, "John, I notice that every afternoon you have difficulty keeping awake. What is your problem?" Well, I was trying to work two full-time jobs. I worked from midnight to eight in the morning building tires, then from eight in the morning to half past four as a time study analyst. I was about twenty minutes late every day. My supervisor and I were the only two white workers in the ingot department. The other eighteen workers were black and I had a lot of fun with them. This department had several overhead cranes to handle the aluminum ingots, which were about twelve feet long and a foot and a half in diameter. Each one weighed about 4,000 lbs. My boss told me that I had to make a decision now as to which job was the one I intended to keep and terminate the other. I kept my tire builder job only because it paid more.

John A. Novobilski

I almost forgot another job that I had during one summer as a caddy at the elite Brookside Country Club in Pottstown. What an experience when my first customer was a local Judge. He would score a 6, 7 or 8 on a hole and he would insist that I mark his score as a 4 or 5. Naturally, I did not argue with him, but my respect for people in the legal field dropped pretty low.

Labor Intensive Industries

The Stowe/Pottstown area had a large number of factories and they employed people from as far away as fifty or sixty miles. At the peak of employment there were up to 5000 people working at these various plants. The property tax base was low because the industries carried the bulk of the tax load. Politicians and unions loved this. They pushed taxes and wages to the breaking point with the obvious result - manufacturers began to look for new places to do business. Guess what? Taxes on individual properties had to be increased as the plants moved out of the area. The real property tax rate in Pottstown climbed to about fifty percent higher than surrounding communities. The shutdown of these plants and the resulting loss of highly paid skilled jobs had a devastating effect on the area's economy. The old philosophy was to quit school and get a factory job to gain seniority as soon as possible. Also, join the union so that they will back you no matter how badly you perform and always complain vociferously to management even if they try to help maintain your job and the position of the company! With the plants moving out and more workers than available jobs, the old philosophy became moot!

Stanley G. Flagg plumbing fittings manufacturing plant was located in Stowe. They had several buildings on an eighty-acre site. They employed about 1,000 craftsmen, laborers, and office workers by the mid 1980's. The last hundred employees were laid off in 1997. The manufacturing of cast iron and galvanized iron plumbing fittings was hot and dirty work. The molder was the key job, and wages were based on production. The laborers, a job my Pop had, moved wheelbarrows full of hot sand from the molders completed castings to a dumping area. Pop was about five-foot-six and weighed about 135 - 140 lbs. at most. He would come home sweaty and smelly and looking totally exhausted. No doubt he wondered at times why he left the Podhale region of southern Poland with its farms on rolling hills, fresh water streams, and wooded forests. He walked to and from work, slightly more than a mile from home. People who lived within fifty or more miles of the plant worked for the company for years.

Gudebrod Knitting mills was located close to Stowe. At its peak the company employed about a hundred knitters, laborers, and office workers. The primary products were knitted clothing.

Doehler (Jarvis) die casting plant was located in Pottstown about four and a half miles from our home. At their wartime peak there were about 600 employees – die makers, casting machine and punch press operators, engineers, clerical workers, and laborers. Engineers and die makers were the highest paid workers. They were responsible for insuring that the finished products met rigid specifications. Originally, the company started as Doehlers. Years later the Jarvis organization joined Doehlers as a partner. The buildings became vacant about 1985 and were later used as warehouses. They burned to the ground on July 15, 2004.

Life of a Greatest Generation Survivor

Bethlehem Steel fabricating plant was also located in Pottstown. They employed as many as 200 people – crane operators, welders, layout technicians, clerks, engineers, and erectors. They fabricated steel beams and plates for bridges and building frames.

Spicer (Dana) automobile parts manufacturing plant is still located at its original site in southeast Pottstown. This plant runs on a three-shift schedule. Our old house is about seven miles from the plant. My brother George and sister Annette worked there. George worked in the centerless grinding department for about seven or eight years. Annette received a fair pension after more than twenty years in the drive shaft department. Some of our friends worked at the plant for as long as forty to forty-five years. It is sad to see much of our manufacturing facilities in the U.S.A. being shut down as we outsource this work to foreign countries. Numerous high paying skilled jobs have been lost, leaving mostly service jobs that pay much less and require minimal skills. Earlier, I discussed what I believe were some of the reasons for the collapse of manufacturing in the Pottstown area and in the U.S.A. as a whole. It should be noted that, on several occasions, a move was started to shut down the Spicer (Dana) plant because of inefficiency that was largely the result of union activities and employee indifference. This plant's operation has been vital to the local economy. At its peak, it employed about a thousand people. Closing it would cause a financial crisis in the town. As Lee Iacocca said in his book, we will end up selling pizza and hamburgers to each other with all of our manufacturing jobs moving overseas to countries with low wages, no environmental controls, and poor working conditions. We just cannot compete with the labor market in countries that use employees as slaves!

New England Auto Parts (NEAPCO) plant is still going strong in Pottstown. At their peak they employed about 300 people – screw machine, lathe and grinding operators, engineers, technicians, laborers, and clerical employees. A couple of my friends worked at the plant, and one was employed there for over thirty-five years.

The old Firestone Tire and Plastics manufacturing plant is still in Pottstown, however, Occidental Chemical Company took over the plant about twenty years ago. At its peak it employed about 1500 people. In my experience working at many jobs and many different facilities, I count the Firestone company as the best for both the working conditions and the company's attitude. As I noted before, I really liked building tires, but I quit my job at the Pottstown plant in September 1947 and hitchhiked to California.

After my second tour of military service ended in 1952 at the El Toro Marine base in California, I applied for a job at the Los Angeles Firestone plant. Would you believe that they hired me the very next day based on my good record in Pottstown? I really needed a good paying job quickly because of our financial situation after, by orders of President Truman, I was dragged back into the Marine Corps to serve a year beyond the expiration of my inactive reserve enlistment. I was a very disgruntled marine by that point. My gung-ho spirit dropped to a low of two from a high of nine. At the time I was attending college full time and had a wife and two children. Meanwhile, some of my classmates who were in the "active" reserves and who had no children were not called back to serve additional time. They were getting paid for active reserve duty – I was not!

Besides the larger factories that I have mentioned here, there were many other small factories in the Pottstown area. The Pottstown Shirt Company employed about fifty workers making men's dress shirts. There were several bakeries that made bread, pastries, pretzels, and potato chips. If you ever bought shoe polish, there is a good chance it was made in Pottstown by the KIWI Co. This company has since moved to a larger more modern plant about five miles west of town. In addition, there were several auto repair agencies in the area, such as Packard, Ford, GMC, Studebaker and others.

The Great Depression

The Great Depression started on Black Tuesday October 29, 1929, when the New York stock market collapsed and it continued until 1941 or 1942 depending on how the economy was in different areas of the country. People born or living in this country prior to 1940 would like to forget this dreadful period. Most people were barely getting by. A job was hard to find. If you had one, you were anxious to keep it. The common slogan was, "brother can you spare a dime?" The soup lines were usually long, but what else was there to do without a job? Hand-me-down clothes were greatly appreciated. I remember when our relatives visited us from New York and Rhode Island we were so excited to get some of their old clothes. These clothes usually had some worn or patched areas. We were embarrassed about it back then, but they actually looked a lot like today's designer clothes. Another benefit of our relatives visiting was getting to ride in their cars. What a thrill! Our family did not own a car until I bought the first one, a 1938 Ford convertible coupe. The only vehicle we had, beside my cart, was a wheelbarrow with a cast iron wheel and steel tube handles. These were the days when Mom would buy a large bag of week-old bread (ten to twelve loaves) for fifty cents. It contained pumpernickel or rye bread, which had a lot of nutrition and it made good onion sandwiches. Friends would evacuate the area!

Life of a Greatest Generation Survivor

Back then, we reused as many things as we could: string, paper bags, and potato and flour sacks. Flour sacks were made into clothes. As I recall, even up to the 1970's they were used to make women's skirts. We used potato sacks to carry "borrowed coal," chickens, grains and many other items. String and paper bags were used over and over until they broke.

One way of taking some pressure off our fuel budget was "knocking off" coal. After midnight, the adult members of the family, would head for the railroad tracks about a mile from home. They kept an eye out for "coal cars" and railroad detectives. When it was safe, they would "knock off" coal to the ground and gather it into potato sacks. Anthracite coal was preferable to bituminous coal. Anthracite coal burned almost smoke free and much hotter than smoke-producing bituminous coal. A couple of older bachelors might trade a few sacks of "borrowed" coal for a pint of potato whiskey or a couple of homemade beers.

Think about the number of toys that children have today. Closets and even whole rooms are filled with every imaginable store-bought toy. In my family, the number of store bought toys was zero. So what did we do? We made our own. Take a dried corncob stick some chicken or goose feathers in one end and a sharp piece of steel in the other end and you now have a toy that whirls when you throw it into the air. Of course, you have to get out of the way when it plummets to the ground. Find a wheel and attach it to a stick about four feet long and you have a one-wheeled cart. Find an old car fender, preferably from a 1932 Ford or Chevrolet, and you have a toboggan. Back when I was a kid, you had to use your imagination. With some thought and scraps of this and that you made your own toys.

There was one item on display in the Woolworth 5 & 10 cent store that I wanted with a passion. It was an aviator's patent-leather cap with chinstraps and goggles. In the fall and winter, I would stop by the store to look at it every chance I got. At $1.99, it was way out of my budget. That money would buy about twenty-five to thirty loaves of week-old bread! Still, I used to dream about someday getting one of those caps.

Unemployment during the Depression peaked at about 25%. Even if you did have a job, the wages were usually very low unless you were a professional. See Tabulation 1 below, which gives a summary of the costs, income, and other data for years shown. It becomes rather clear that inflation has been running wild for a number of years. The net effect is that the more people earn the more they have to spend for food and material things. It should be noted that labor unions keep the workers stirred up to get wage increases, meanwhile, other countries are able to sell their products at a lower cost. As a result, U.S. factories shutdown and jobs are lost. This creates a vicious circle of economic movement that ends where?

Did you ever hear a union representative or environmentalist (Budget Buster) admit that they were partly to blame for our industries out sourcing? Because of their demands on our industries it is impossible to be competitive with other countries that have little or no regard for their employees, the environment, safety, decent wages and product safety.

Life of a Greatest Generation Survivor

TABULATION ONE

ITEM/ YEAR	1925	1943	1995	2005
1 – Average Income/yr.$	2,200	2,000	26,000	40,000
2 – New Car - $	290	900	15,000	20,000
3 – New House - $	7,800	3,600	100,000	180,000
4 – Bread - Loaf – Cents	9	10	150	250
5 – Milk – Gallon - Cents	56	62	240	350
6 - Gasoline-Gallon-Cents	12	15	125	300
7 – Gold – Ounce - $	20.7	35	377	420
8 – Dow-Jones -Average-$	134	134	5,117	11,000
9 – Life Expectancy – Years	54.1	62.9	76.3	79.2

Obviously, there was much unrest among labor due to the unfair behavior of many corporations. I agree that unions were necessary based on what happened to my Pop at S. G. Flagg Company, but in later years the pendulum swung the other way. The unions gained too much power with negative results for employers and employees.

The Great Depression was hard for all. Churches, The Salvation Army and various civic organizations tried to assist poor families. Many people spent their time scouring dumps and visiting soup kitchens. In both cases the pickings were slim. In 1935, by Executive Order, President Roosevelt created the WPA (Works Projects Administration or cynically called, We Poke Along) to assist families by providing jobs and wages for goods and supplies. Eventually, there were 8.5 million workers at work in 1.4 million projects throughout the country.

John A. Novobilski

So what were some of the lessons I learned from the Great Depression?

A) Live below your means–save a little for unexpected needs – not wants!

B) Strive to be debt free – pay with cash as often as possible. (Credit cards have ruined many people in today's economy.)

C) Put your savings in insured bank accounts.

D) Own a home – with a little plot of ground for growing food.

E) Maintain emergency reserves like food, cash, clothes, etc.

F) Be careful with investments. There are a lot of "sharks" ready to relieve you of your life savings! There are NO free lunches.

G) Avoid waste of food, energy resources such as electricity, gasoline and natural gas, clothes and time.

H) Just because the neighbor has it does not mean that you can afford it. Or that you need it!

World War II

Due to years of political isolationism, in 1940 the U.S. military was low on equipment and trained personnel. On September 16, 1940 President Roosevelt signed the first peace time military "draft," and all men aged twenty-one to thirty-five were required to register. On November 13, 1942 President Roosevelt expanded that age range to include all men between eighteen and thirty-five. Thanks to the combined efforts of industry, labor, the military and the public, our country geared up in record time to help our allies – Great Britain, France and Russia. Later, Italy switched from siding with Hitler to joining the allies.

Japanese fleet commander and wartime leader Admiral Isoruku Yamamoto (1884 – 1943) was a Harvard graduate and familiar with U.S. might. It was his opinion that a war against America would be impossible to win. However, he did plan the attack on Pearl Harbor. This attack, on December 7, 1941, triggered the U.S.A. and Great Britain to declare war on Japan the next day. Yamamoto never lived to see the final result of the war against the U.S.A., which ended in September 1945. Our intelligence group broke the Japanese code and determined that he would be flying to Bougainville to visit his troops. On April 18, 1943 a group of Army Air Force P-38 Lightening planes shot down

Yamamoto's plane. His death was a tremendous blow to the Japanese military.

Sixteen million Americans served in the military during World War II. They fought in the European Theatre against Germany and Italy, and in the Pacific Theatre against the Japanese Empire. In 2007 *only about 2.5 million, or 15 %, of World War II veterans are still alive, and the survivor list is getting smaller daily.* In addition to those serving in the military, the people at home were busy collecting scrap materials and making products necessary for the front line warriors. Since so much food was required by the military, these home front warriors were subject to severe rationing. It was the greatest display of cooperation and commitment to a goal of total victory – a feat that cannot be equaled.

(It would be great if our "do nothing" congress could act the way they did back then to attend to the numerous problems we have today starting with Energy Independence! Other problems are shown later.)

From 1941 to 1943 I was attending my last two years at Pottstown High School. Our school in Stowe, West Pottsgrove Junior High, which I graduated from in June 1941, had classes from the first through the tenth grades only. As I described earlier, I lettered in football and basketball at West Pottsgrove. Then, at Pottstown High, four classmates and I formed the Trojan bowling team in 1941 – 42. We competed with other schools, especially those in the Philadelphia area. We paid for our own alley and equipment costs, and because of our success, the school eventually assigned a teacher to monitor our contests. We ultimately won the State of Pennsylvania championship. We were treated to an all expenses paid trip to Columbus, Ohio to bowl against Ohio school teams and mingle with the bowlers in the American Bowling Congress competition. These were professional bowlers from the U.S.A. and other countries competing for prize money and awards. I had never been so far away from home. It was pretty overwhelming. See DOCUMENT 8 & 8A, clippings from the Pottstown Mercury about the Pottstown High Bowling team, and DOCUMENT 9, my Bowling Award Letter. DOCUMENT 9A is a tribute to Pottstown High School Class of 1943, which I presented at our 2003 Reunion.

In 1942 my brother George joined the Navy and became a member of the 110th Construction Battalion (C B's), generally referred to as the "SeaBees." PICTURE 12 shows George in Hawaii in January of 1944. The Seabees were, for the most part, a group of older men - experienced machinists, welders, mechanics, carpenters, surveyors, riggers, and electricians. Many of the Seabees treated us younger Marines as though they were our fathers. Their battalions provided military units with buildings, electrical and water supply systems, mess halls, etc. George was stationed on Tinian Island when the Air Force was training to make the B-29 run on Japan to drop atomic bombs. These operations were isolated from other military and civilian actions and kept secret.

John A. Novobilski

PICTURE 12 – *George Walter Nobilski (shortened name), 2nd Class Machinist Mate, 110th Seabees. Hawaii, January 1944—Served on Tinian Island near Saipan and Guam.*

I was sworn into the Marine Corps on October 18, 1943 and I reported to Boot Camp at Parris Island, South Carolina on November 1, 1943. Imagine a six-foot-tall 163-pound kid going into the Marine Corps. A government study made in later years determined that there were so many undernourished kids entering the service, something had to be done for future children. This was the original inspiration for the school lunch program, which now includes breakfast, too! I was assigned to Platoon 821, which had about seventy new recruits. I still remember my rifle number – 1611991. Many of us were from the northeast and had Polish and Italian names. Our Drill Instructor (DI) was from the south and he had a hard time pronouncing our names. He was used to names like Williams, Jones, Miller, Baxter, Scroggs, Hawk, Hager, Crow, Jenkins, and Bird.

So why did I join the Marine Corps? Here are a few reasons why I enlisted instead of being drafted into the Army.

> 1) The challenge. The word was that it was tough to complete basic training and earn the title US Marine.
> 2) My cousin Steve, whom I had great respect for because of his athletic prowess in baseball, football,

track, polevault, etc., joined in 1934. He was a Gunnery Sergeant in the Battle of Guadalcanal and his leadership abilities were recognized. With leaders being killed so often, he was given a "spot" commission to 2nd Lieutenant. This was the first of many island battles against the Japanese between August 7, 1942 and February 8, 1943. Also, my cousin Dickie joined the Marine Corps in 1942. He rose to the rank of Master Sergeant. Dickie had helped me learn how to swim, fish, trap animals, play baseball, football and do many other things during my younger years. I was forever grateful to him. Before he passed away in 1986, I let him know how much I appreciated the guidance he had given me in my formative years. I remember that he responded with a smile of satisfaction.

3) In Stowe, we had a number of guys who enlisted in the corps. One family had five brothers – John, Ray, Willie, Steve and Eddie - who joined and fought against the Japanese all over the Pacific. I admired their dedication and courage. Eddie was training to become a Drill Instructor at Parris Island when I was in boot camp. He visited with me once for about an hour. I did not see him again until we both served as grooms at my sister's wedding in 1946.

4) I had no desire to be in the Navy cooped up on a ship, and the Army and Air Force did not seem to fit my goals.

While on the trip from Stowe/Pottstown, I had to change trains in Philadelphia so I stopped to use the restroom. I laid my watch on the counter to wash my hands then turned around to get some paper towels. When I turned back to get my watch, a gift for high school graduation from my sister

John A. Novobilski

Levina, IT WAS GONE! You can tell how "green" and trusting this young guy was on his first big trip. This was a truly sad experience – learning the ways of the big city and real world. So we arrive in Yamassee, S.C. where we transfer to a bus, which takes us to Parris Island. This will be our home for ten weeks with no contact with the outside world except by mail. Scurrying to get off the bus and fall into ranks looked and felt like the proverbial Chinese fire drill. Many of the recruits were confused and looked around in amazement as if to say, "What the hell am I doing here?" Individualism was a bunch of crap and it was not tolerated in the Marine Corps. We quickly learned to do things as a team. To me it was a new and exciting experience, and I soon found that the food was very good. I could not understand why some of the "boots" were complaining. I'd never had it so good. We even had free dental and medical services. Well, not really free, since we only made about fifty dollars per month. This amounts to about twenty-eight cents per hour for a forty-hour week. However, it was actually about eighty-four hours a week, which is about fourteen cents per hour. Still, there is much more to the Marine Corps than money: the clean living, daily exercise, nutritious food and pride of accomplishment which one experiences there is hard to put a price on. The daily challenges kept us physically and mentally focused on realistic goals.

As youngsters growing up in Stowe we learned the five R's – readin', 'ritin, 'rithmetic, *respect and responsibility.* These R's made Boot Camp go much easier because we understood respect for authority and we were responsible for our actions! Sadly, we had recruits in our platoon that had difficulty getting into the rhythm of training because of their indifference to responsibility and lack of respect for others. The long days of exercises, marching, hiking, classroom and field instruction required focus or penalties would result. When one boot goofed up the whole platoon could suffer. On the obstacle course, one recruit in our platoon fell off a horizontal rope while trying to traverse a water hole – plop into the water he goes. The penalty? He had to sit in a tree twenty-five feet above ground from 1700 to 2200 hours while singing "I'm a shit bird from Yamassee, a bigger shit bird you'll never see" over and over again. Those who could not or would not keep up with the blistering pace were left behind in a special slower paced platoon or they were discharged. There were a few who faked mental and physical illness to get out of the Marine Corps, even if it meant a dishonorable discharge. Also, in the marines we had to clean our barracks or Quonset huts and the area around the buildings. Dive-bombing was a specific assignment, which entailed wielding a stick with a sharp nail on the end to spear cigarette butts and place the butts in a bag. Personal clothes were scrubbed, washed and hung out to dry. There was no laundry service, and Momma was not allowed on the base to wash Junior's clothes. What a travesty of justice for the rich kids. Since everyone's clothes were the same except for size, all clothes had to be stamped with the owner's name. Theft of clothes was difficult and resulted in a stiff penalty. The Marine Corps did not tolerate marines stealing from one another. Now, if it meant taking something from the Army, Navy, or Coast Guard, it was merely a case of borrowing. My good friend from Rochester, New York "borrowed" a JEEP from the Army, and we used it on Okinawa for several months.

The obstacle course and the water events tested your mettle. If you made it through, there was a deep sense of accomplishment and pride in your platoon. At the rifle range one could do very well if he paid attention to the knowledgeable instructors. One "ole hillbilly boy" named Lange, from Tennessee, gave me a bad time before and during the rifle range qualifications. He told me that he was going to "whip my ass" because he was such a good shot. He had shot rabbits and squirrels from a young age, while I had never even held a rifle. Well, on qualification day for the Garand M-1 Rifle, I made Sharpshooter and he made Marksman. The highest rank was Expert, then Sharpshooter and finally Marksman! Lange never talked to me again. I do not know where he was assigned after boot camp. I do know that he should have listened to the instructors. I did and it was the right choice.

I shall never forget the popular song "It Had to Be You". As we were marching at a snappy pace, four abreast, our Assistant D.I. was counting cadence – ah on top treep, ah on top treep, (meaning left, right, left, right) while our D.I. was singing the song. Evidently, I must have been listening to the song and I got out step with the rest of the troops. Without warning, the D.I. cracks his baton on my head – WHACK ! To this day, I cannot forget the two- It Had to Be You and WHACK !

We were given a number of aptitude tests in Boot Camp to assist officers in making individual assignments. Some of us volunteered to be placed in specific units based on our experience or desire for certain types of work or technical classifications. I wanted to serve as a paratrooper. However, attempts to drop paratroop forces on the pacific islands were a failure. These units were abolished and the crews used to prepare food, equipment, and ammunition for parachute drops to the front line units. Some of the guys were assigned to cooks and bakers' school, the infantry, sea duty, aviation and other duties. My aptitude tests indicated a talent for technical work, so I was assigned to aviation. I was glad that cooking and baking was not in my future. Also, sea duty seemed like a boring way to spend a military career - as a guard on a ship, cooped up in small quarters, with little to accomplish. As you will see later, even as a marine my days aboard ship were too numerous and I did not like it!

When we graduated from boot camp, we got to go home on a ten-day furlough. See PICTURE 13. I was promoted to Private First Class (PFC), one chevron stripe – big deal. However, I had also earned "THE TITLE" as described below:

THE TITLE
It can not be inherited
Nor can it ever be purchased.
You and no one alive
Can buy it at any price;
It is impossible to rent
and it cannot be lent;
You alone and our own
have earned it
with your sweat, and blood and lives;
you own it forever;
The Title
"UNITED STATES MARINE"

PICTURE 13 - *PFC John A. Novobilski January 1944 —After "Boot Camp" in Platoon 821 at Parris, Island, S.C. Note Sharpshooter Medal for Garand M-1 Rifle qualification + other ladder of medals. With active & reserve time I served 7 yr. & 4 mo. in the U.S. Marines.*

This was the time to show our stuff and make the rounds of girlfriends, old stomping grounds, and former work places. It was in the cold of mid winter, though, and getting around was rough without a car. The buses took forever and cabs cost too much. After my furlough, I was off to Cherry Point, North Carolina in an old smoke-belching train. After a short stay at Cherry Point, a few of us were assigned to the Naval Air Technical Training Center (NATTC) in Memphis, Tennessee for aviation mechanic and gunner training. See PICTURE 14.

PICTURE 14 -
John A Novobilski
At NATTC
Memphis, TN
June 1944

The others went off to become "mud marines" by training at Camp Lejeune in North Carolina or Camp Pendleton in California. When I think of the whole process now, the logistics of running the war was monumental. It took a lot of good managerial skills to keep the many diverse activities on target. The planning and organization needed was very challenging. Even so, there were some hurry-up-and-wait periods to allow for errors and adjustments.

Life of a Greatest Generation Survivor

While stationed at NATTC, we were trained to adjust controls and make repairs on planes from propeller to tail and wing tip to wing tip. It was important to know a little about guns, rockets, torpedoes, and bombs. We participated in various forms of exercises, fire drills, marching, and barracks clean up. A group of us guys between six-foot and six-foot-five formed a drill team. We performed at parades and other ceremonial events. You should have heard the click of heels at the different commands – like rifle shots – as we marched to the music of John Phillip Sousa.

During our exercise time we were scheduled to box against a classmate. One day I was slated to box against my friend Joe from Pittsburgh. Early in the first round, I hit him with a left hook and something flew out of his mouth – we didn't use mouthpieces. He had a partial replacement, but I did not know people were fitted with such dental devices. It scared the hell out of me. I thought he was terribly injured. Then he explained about the partial and we had a good laugh.

Transportation from NATTC, located in Millington, to Memphis was provided by a Navy "cattle car"- a large trailer with rows of benches pulled by a tractor unit – at no cost to us marines and sailors. It was about twenty miles from NATTC to Memphis. In any event, one day my friend from Philadelphia, Alberto Phillipo Schifalaqua and I, John Albert Novobilski made a blind date with a couple of Memphis Belles. We met the ladies in front of a drug store close by the well-known Peabody Hotel. When they learned our full names they literally split their guts with laughter. They thought we were kidding and that no one could ever have such names. Eventually they settled down and the evening went by fine. I kept dating Ida Mae, and she wrote to me frequently while I was overseas. During this time, she also wrote to my sister Angie. I will discuss more about Ida Mae when I get to my return home from Okinawa.

Graduation to AMM (Aviation Machinist Mate) at NATTC came on June 23, 1944. I advanced to Corporal – two stripes. On July 8, 1944 my class boarded a train for a 1,800-mile cross-country trip to the Miramar Naval Air Station near San Diego, California. There we goofed off while awaiting our next assignment. We were permitted to spend liberty in close by La Jolla (beautiful and for the rich only town with a Pacific Ocean view), Los Angeles, or San Diego. On one liberty trip two buddies and I hitchhiked to Los Angeles. We made the rounds walking north on Hill Street. When we reached the intersection of 4th and Hill we were accosted by three or four Navy Military Police. Actually, I was heading into a corner drugstore to buy cigarettes. The Navy Police accused us of not saluting a Naval Officer. It was a sting – entrapment. Where were you ACLU loons when we needed you to fight our case? We did not get any brig (jail) time since we shipped out overseas before there was any kind of hearing. By coincidence, ten years later almost to the day, I would be working as a mechanical engineer in an office located at that same corner.

The time has come for us to climb aboard the USAT Sea Ray troop ship on August 8, 1944. The ship was waiting for us at the San Diego harbor. I was still only eighteen and my birthday would come on August 15. We did not know our destination. We arrived at Espiritu Santo, New Hebrides Island on August 27. The ship had zigzagged all the way, and no lights were allowed topside as a precaution to enemy discovery. The entire trip took nineteen days and covered 5000 miles. On an Army-run troop ship, every cubic foot of space is used. We were packed like sardines – our narrow bunks arranged side by side, end to end, and about six or seven high. Many of the guys got sick as dogs. There was sweat and vomit all over the place. When we crossed the equator, those guys who had never crossed before underwent a crude initiation. Neptunus Rex and his workers smeared us with enamel paint in sensitive places. It was impossible to get the paint off in saltwater showers. The lavatories sat in four or five inches of filthy water. We had no paint thinner available to remove the paint from ourselves. I went up to the Officers Deck to borrow a helmet full of fresh water. Well, a young officer caught me. He was going to put me on report. I would possibly get some brig time. However, an older officer came by and told the junior officer to forget the incident and turn me loose. I went below with the water. This was the first time that I really thought about the way officers were treated compared to non –commissioned personnel. I do not think that officers should have had as many privileges as they did, while the troops were treated like 2nd or 3rd class citizens. *We were all there working toward a common goal.* I learned then and there that it was essential to go to college and get a degree - regardless of the type – basket weaving, arts, playing sports or whatever. It took me thirteen years to eventually earn an engineering degree by attending a lot of night classes. I will be forever grateful for the G.I. Bill of

John A. Novobilski

Rights, signed on June 22, 1944 by President Roosevelt. Kids from my background never expected to attend and graduate from college. My Pottstown High School class had 237 students and only about three or four percent went on to graduate from college. So it was quite an achievement for this Stowe kid to get an engineering degree after such a poor performance in high school.

Also on this trip, we crossed the International Dateline where the date west of it was one day ahead of that on the east side. Refer to DOCUMENT 10 MAP which shows the route of all travel by troop transport from San Diego, California, to the south and north Pacific and back to Los Angeles – definitely not the luxury way to travel.

New Hebrides is about 150 miles northwest of the Fiji Islands. On this island we became part of the Red Devil Squadron VMTB 232. We were trained by the old veterans from the Guadalcanal campaign on Grumman or General Motors TBF or TBM Avenger torpedo bombers. The crew included: Pilot, Turret Gunner and Rear Gunner/Radioman. See PICTURE 15 showing the Avenger. The island had lagoons like those in the "Tarzan" movies of the 1940s. They were crystal clear and we got good workouts by swinging from vines and diving into the deep water. After about a month of training, we boarded the USAT Cape Cleare troop ship on September 23. Our next destination was the Ulithi Atoll, about 2800 miles northwest from New Hebrides, for more training with a full squadron of about 450 personnel.

PICTURE 15 - *TBF Grumman AVENGER used by "Red Devil" Squadron VMTB 232 beginning in 1942. Top Speed 278 mph. Armor: Wings have 50 caliber machine gun and Turret 50 caliber with Rear 30 caliber machine guns. Carries: 1-2,000 lb. Torpedo or bomb or 4 – 500 lb bombs. Engine is 1,900 Horsepower.*

We disembarked on the small island of Falalop as part of the 2nd wave invasion of the Ulithi Atoll on October 22. By the way, we had to borrow a tent from an Army communications outfit. Our supplies had not arrived. This caused a ruckus between our squadron leaders and the Army leaders. Eventually peace was declared and we had our new tent. From this island we were able to bomb and strafe the Japanese-held island of Yap. It was very hot on Falalop and our dress code was: shorts made from chopped off khaki trousers, no shirt, "boon docker" shoes cut away to make them air cooled, and an official USMC cap. By then we had traveled forty-nine days and about 8,000 miles by troop transport.

John A. Novobilski

The invasion of Okinawa was set for Sunday April 1, 1945. This was to be the bloodiest of any battle and was fought by the largest U.S. fleet utilized during the war. Japanese suicide missions, known popularly as "kamikaze attacks," were overwhelming and destructive to our naval fleet and land operations. Okinawa is located about 350 miles from the Japanese mainland. The island is sixty-five miles long and ranges from five to fifteen miles in width. DOCUMENT 11 shows the island of Okinawa, which would serve as the base for the pending attack on the Japanese homeland. This was a battle the Japanese people and their leaders did not want to lose; they were ready to sacrifice everyone to engage the mighty U.S.A.

Our Squadron's first and second echelon landed on the island on April 4 and 6 respectively. The landings on the west coast were relatively easy for the infantry and our units. This was much to everyone's surprise, since the Japanese were waiting in the many caves south of the Shuri Castle. We in the third echelon boarded the USS Sherburne (APA 205) on April 10. This was a 1600-mile trip and meant twenty more days of suffering aboard a troop transport ship. By the end of this trip we could consider ourselves experienced Navy swab jockeys. This is just what I tried to avoid by enlisting in the Marines. Thus far we had been on the seas for about seventy days traveling almost 10,000 miles. Certainly this was much more Navy time than the "desk hardened" Navy officers and enlisted swabbies back in the states put in. I knew and worked with some of them after WWII was over. Some had real easy rackets.

On our way to Okinawa, we stopped at the Guam harbor

Life of a Greatest Generation Survivor

on April 16. We stayed there four days, but had to stay on board the ship or only swim nearby. My pent up energy drove me to dive off the ship's bow - about twenty-five feet above the surface of the water. Wow, I thought I would never reach water. When I finally made contact my head almost exploded because my arms and hands did not break the water. A couple of other guys reluctantly followed my dare. We were not injured, though, and waiting in the chow line was our next challenge.

After we left the Guam harbor, our troop transport ship passed by Tinian. I was unaware at the time that my brother George was stationed on Tinian. The islands of Tinian, Guam, and Saipan are close together and our forces captured them from the Japanese in 1944. We finally left Saipan on April 27 and arrived on Okinawa May 1, 1945. Our squadron now consisted of fifty-six officers and 320 enlisted men. Meanwhile, the 1st and 6th Marine divisions and Army units were engaged in fierce battles against the Japanese forces tunneled in a honeycomb of caves in the south. A close friend from Stowe, Mike, was in the 1st Marine division mortar section in the battle on the Shuri line. A few of us went to visit him close to the Shuri castle and the hills where the Japanese were in a network of caves – like an underground city.

Our squadron had tents and a mess hall rather close to the main Kadena aircraft runway. We built foxholes close by for quick and ready access when the enemy bombs, shells, and rockets or kamikaze planes were heading to our area. The occupants of each tent, usually six men, built their own foxhole. Teamwork was the order of the day and goof offs were ostracized. Our twenty-four planes were parked on compacted coral revetments a couple of miles from the living area. I was assigned to the engineering section – we were responsible for the overhaul and major repairs or replacements of engines, propellers, landing gear and other parts. This entailed the dismantling of parts, cleaning them with aviation gasoline, assembly and testing as required. After several weeks at this job, I requested to work on the Line as an assistant to a plane crew chief. We were responsible for running the plane for a check of the various devices prior to flight by the pilot and crew. Since our gunner positions were fully staffed, our opportunity to fly as gunners was limited. See PICTURE 16, which shows the squadron line crews.

PICTURE 16 - *VMTB 232 Line crews on Okinawa June 1945. See John with Buddies Hardy, Moore, Harrah, Gwiazda, et.al.*

Life of a Greatest Generation Survivor

The ordinance group was responsible for preparation, handling and installation of bombs and torpedoes in the bomb bay, 50 caliber ammunition for the wing and turret mounted guns and 30 caliber ammunition for the rear machine gun.

Now for my perspective on WAR: War is an equal opportunity, non-discriminatory event, except for draft dodgers like Bill Clinton. Military and civilian people caught in battles are wounded physically and mentally, maimed or killed without regard to their station on earth. One's ethnicity, religion, color or sex does not matter. It also doesn't matter whether one is on the ground, on or under the sea, or in the air. We had privates and generals and all ranks in between get wounded or lose their lives. Let me tell you when you realize that you are in a war: when the first bullet, shell, rocket or bomb is heading in your direction and you have little or no control over the end results. The enemy is trying to kill you! This is War. During enemy attacks, most people fear for their lives. The "Hollywood Rambo's" of the movies are a myth. Most normal guys are not cavalier about going into battle.

I had a few stained skivvies (under shorts) events on Okinawa. Every evening at dusk, Pistol Pete (the name we gave the Japs who used to send shells our way) launched a few shells at our area. It so happened that on May 6 I was tired of sleeping with my clothes on so I hit the sack buck naked with my shoes and helmet close by. Suddenly, here come the shells, with their unique, easily recognized whistling and whirring sound. Off I go flying toward the foxhole with my helmet and shoes in my hands. I slid into the foxhole on my butt and received a few scratches. After the shelling ended, we went to check the damage. One shell had hit close to our tent and shrapnel flew through the exact spot where my head would have been resting – my quick action had saved my life. The other guys made it to the foxhole and were safe. A couple hundred feet away, though, four crew members were hit by shrapnel. A Master Sergeant had been hit by shrapnel, which penetrated his mouth and jaw – his jaw hung down like a flap. He was transported to a hospital ship. The other three men were treated by our squadron doctor and released for duty. I never heard how the Master Sergeant recuperated. The scratches on my butt were insignificant.

On May 16, while providing support to our front line troops one of our planes was hit by a 40mm enemy shell. The Turret Gunner was hurt and he bailed out over the front line. He was rescued by men from the 1st Marine Division. Co-operation and protection of one another was primary and it was remarkable to see it in action. The Radio Gunner was hurt and passed out as the pilot was lining up the plane for a crash landing about a hundred feet above the runway. The Radio Gunner then jumped to his death. It was an awful sight – this is war.

About a week later, on May 24, I was assigned to guard duty at the Yontan (Yomitan) Airfield. At about 10 PM, thirteen Japanese bombers were trying to land and destroy our aircraft. They flew in under our radar, but by other tracking methods our U.S. forces were aware of their objectives. Anti-aircraft fire knocked out at least seven of the planes and one landed close to our parked aircraft. The hail of fire from anti-aircraft guns and rifles manned by myself and other guards was so dangerous that poking your head out of a foxhole could be the end. See PICTURE 17 for an idea of the firepower being displayed. Keep in mind that there are four or five live bullets for every tracer.

PICTURE 17 – *Anti-aircraft and rifle fire tracer's shower when Japs landed a "Sally" bomber on Yontan airfield.*

The enemy crash-landed the one shot up Jap "Sally" plane. A dozen commandos on board went scurrying around our planes throwing demolition charges. Ultimately, they were all killed. See PICTURE 18, the crashed plane. Our planes were on fire. Due to a lack of proper fire-fighting equipment and concern over the possibility of more attacks, the fires raged on until the early morning. The enemy destroyed or damaged twenty-seven planes and large quantities of aviation fuel and munitions. There were no further attempts by the Japanese to land troops on Okinawa.

On June 1, 1945 we had fifty-one officers and 313 enlisted men. Our squadron received letters of commendation for the support we gave the front line marines and army units from: Major General Pedro del Valle, Commander- 1st Marine division; General Hodge, 24th Army Corps-383rd

Army Infantry; and L.E. Woods, Commanding General-2nd Marine Aircraft Wing. Also, we were awarded a Presidential Unit Citation with two stars. We were a "gung-ho" team from the U.S.A. See DOCUMENT 12, 19 August 1945 Commendation Letter.

PICTURES 18 – *Flattened Jap "Betty" Bomber — Raid of May 24, 1945.*

Another frightening incident occurred on June 16. While I was on guard duty in the area where we parked our planes, I heard a sound like a washing machine motor overhead. A Japanese Mitsubishi bomber was advancing in my direction. What was I going to do with a rifle against an enemy bomber? As the bomber sound, ah-ah-ah-ah, got closer, the first bomb was released and I could have sworn that it was about to drop on me. Then bombs two, three, and four fell. I thought for sure that number four had my name on it, as I lay prostrate on the hard coral revetment. Sure enough, number four dropped within twenty feet of my position. I felt the shock and the coral debris and shrapnel flying everywhere. I never got a scratch. HE was watching over the gangly kid from Stowe. However, three of our planes were hit with minor damage. The incendiary bomb fragments started to burn the planes. I quickly doused the fires with CO_2 extinguishers, which were always kept close by. The next morning the Sergeant of the Guard drove out in his jeep to check the bombing damage. When he saw me, his first comment was "What are you doing here? We all thought you were a goner." The guy was an old time marine whose name I will never forget – Angus T. Gillis. He gave me a pat on the back (for my courage, I guess) and hurried me to the mess hall for breakfast - no waiting in line. War and survival!

I had some other close calls, but when you are young, dumb, and feel as invincible as many of us did you become lucky. That is the basic reason why the military services like to have young, unmarried and active guys who can be easily molded into warriors by "gung ho" old timers. In our outfit we had some older married men who were caught in the draft. They were more cautious and approached situations with greater trepidation than the young, single guys. I learned a lot from these older guys during the campaign and especially while on liberty. See PICTURES 19 and 20, which show the "Jeep" my friend Clovis, from Rochester, NY borrowed from the Army – and Typhoon damage to our tent area.

PICTURES 19 and 20 – *The JEEP and its proud owner and Typhoon damage. The tents were dumped into rice paddies! Oh well, just another bad day at the office.*

Kamikaze attacks continued daily and the Navy ships took a terrible beating. On the radio we tuned into the propaganda fed to us each evening by Tokyo Rose. Her real name was Iva Toguri. She would start her broadcasts by playing popular recordings such as: Kiss me Once and Kiss me Twice ---, Let's Dance, It Had to be You, You Made me Love You, In the Mood, Missed the Saturday Dance, Moonlight Serenade, Don't Get Around Much Anymore and others. Her favorite messages were:

1) Tonight, you Maleens (that is how she pronounced "Marines") will be gassed and die. So look for the attack. (Note: The Japanese had difficulty pronouncing R's and L's. Chevrolet was very hard – sounded like Shevoray).
2) To all of you married Maleens, tonight your wife is out partying with a rich defense 4 F (exempt from service duty) worker. You are forgotten.
3) To all of you single Maleens, your girlfriend is having the time of her life with a new boyfriend on every date.
4) Listen all of you men. Very soon you will get a "Dear John" letter to let you know that your wife or girlfriend will dump you when and if you get back home.
5) The people back home are living well with lots of money, drinks, cars and food. To them, your dedication is a lost cause.

Today's Democratic Party members are making similar statements about Iraq. Senator Harry Reid of Nevada is leading the charge that "the War in Iraq is Lost." Joining him are Kennedy, Biden, Boxer, Murtha, Dodd and others.

Tokyo Rose was the American-born daughter of Japanese

parents. After the war she pleaded with the U.S. government to spare her, saying that she was held in Japan against her will and forced to spread propaganda for the Japanese hierarchy. She was tried for treason and undermining U.S. troop morale and received a ten-year sentence. However, President Ford pardoned her in 1977. I, along with many others who served in the battle for Okinawa, never understood why he made such a decision considering the terrible propaganda she spread!

Even though the capture of Okinawa ended on June 22, 1945 there was more action. On July 3 our ammunition dump was set afire (why they didn't wait till the 4th?) and the explosions continued all day and into the night of July 4th. Our area of operation was about five miles away and there was no local damage. Was it sabotage? We never did know. We had additional crashes and lost planes. Most of the crews were rescued. One crew was lost when their plane was hit by enemy fire from a small island close to Okinawa. All three men were deemed missing in action – MIAs. They were never found dead or alive. War is an equal opportunity event.

During the battles for the Philippines, Iwo Jima and Okinawa, there were about 2,300 Japanese aircraft involved in kamikaze attacks from October 1944 to mid August 1945. The most severe attacks against the U.S.A. were around Okinawa since this was so close to their homeland. Kamikaze attacks sank thirty-six combat ships. In addition, 368 ships were damaged. The largest ships sunk were three escort carriers, thirteen destroyers, and one destroyer escort. Several U.S. aircraft carriers were knocked out of operation, but none was sunk. Our use of wooden decks on carriers made them vulnerable to great damage.

John A. Novobilski

During the eighty-three day battle for Okinawa, there were 49,000 U.S. casualties – more than in any other campaign in the Pacific. The Marine Corps had 2,938 killed and 13,700 wounded and a few missing. The Army lost 4,580 killed, 93 missing and 18,100 wounded. With the majority of kamikaze attacks aimed at the Navy, they had 4,900 killed and 4,800 wounded. Also, more than 110,000 Japanese military and civilians were killed and 7,400 were taken prisoner.

Around August 18, 1945, I was promoted to sergeant (three stripes) and my pay increased to seventy-eight dollars a MONTH. So, this gangly kid from Stowe is now a big "gung ho Sarge" and only twenty years old.

Japan accepted unconditional surrender on August 14, 1945. When we got the word, all hell broke loose with rifles, machine guns, and other weapons being fired into the air. We U.S. troops were full of joy, happiness and relief. We were anxious to get home and out of this mess. As a result of the gunfire there was some property damage, and even a few injuries, but no one really cared! The official Japanese surrender occurred on September 2, 1945, aboard the battleship Missouri in Tokyo Bay. President Harry S. Truman proclaimed it V-J Day – Victory over Japan!

It was President Truman's decision to drop atomic bombs on Hiroshima and Nagasaki on August 6 and 9 respectively. His decision was a tough one, but the proper one since Japan was willing to sacrifice their men, women and children to wipe out thousands of our troops if we invaded their homeland. If one thinks that the nuclear attack by the USA was wrong – remember *The Japs started the war at Pearl*

Life of a Greatest Generation Survivor

Harbor on December 7, 1941 while they had diplomats in our capitol falsely claiming to be negotiating for peace.

Now that hostilities with Japan were over, we had to battle with Mother Nature. Typhoons struck the island on September 16 and October 9. There were winds of 120 to 140 miles per hour and rains pelted down at forty-five degree angles splattered the island for hours. Mud stuck to everything, especially our shoes – we became four to five inches taller. This was probably where the idea for elevator shoes originated! Our tent was flipped over like a pancake and right into a rice paddy, along with our cots, clothes, seabags, lanterns, helmets and any pictures, books, and manuals. Oh well, life goes on. At least there were no more shells screaming at us. PICTURE 20 shows some of the Typhoon's devastation.

On October 23, 1945 our squadron received orders to return to the good old U.S.A. and be decommissioned. For some reason, they did not reserve a luxury ship for the return trip! So, on October 30, we boarded the APA-220 Okanogan and departed from the totally devastated and flattened island of Okinawa on October 31. From November 1 to 15 we were at sea in the North Pacific. The Captain set the course on a route that was to be the shortest distance between two points - 6,000 miles. Refer to Map shown on DOCUMENT 10. This time there would be no zigzagging. It was full speed ahead. We were going home – what could be better? About 200 miles from our destination, one of the troops mumbled to a few of us that he was going to jump overboard. We thought he was joking so we chuckled and went on talking. We paid no more attention to the guy. A few minutes later here comes the guy running at full speed with a "Mae West" float on and overboard he goes into the ocean. It was dark out, so the floodlights went on, the alarms sounded, and the engines stopped. The search lasted several hours, but he was never found. A report on the incident later concluded he was killed after being pulled into the propellers before the engines were stopped. Also, we found out later that he had received a "Dear John" letter from his wife while on Okinawa, and he could not face the homecoming. Looks like that lousy Tokyo Rose was right in this case. War is Hell!

We arrived at Terminal Island, near San Pedro, California on November 15, 1945. With this trip on the high seas completed, I had been aboard troop transport ships for eighty-six days and traveled more than 15,500 miles – this sure looks like Navy time. You know, twenty-two years later I was the Manager in Charge of one of four large electric generating stations built between 1943 and 1948 in San Pedro. After arrival, we got aboard trucks and headed for the Miramar Naval Base from where we had departed in August 1944. We had been overseas 460 days or more than fifteen months. What an experience for the naïve, green kid from Stowe. There was so much travel, so much action, so much water, so much destruction, so much suffering on both sides. Yet there were also many fun times that made life enjoyable. And, we got back on our own power and without any injuries. We were lucky. I have the greatest respect for the guys who gave their lives or were permanently injured fighting for our great country. Here I was a twenty-year-old war veteran ordering drinks at bars in San Diego where the drinking age was twenty-one. We used to spend time in the local bowling alleys to have fun and raise hell. On more then one occasion, I used to start my approach back as far as possible, running at warp speed and let the ball fly about half way down the alley. The alley manager did not appreciate this. He would ask us to leave or call the police. We were a bunch of cocky wise guys and stupid, too! I can still remember the first time that I got drunk. We got back to the barracks about midnight and the bunk was in a spin. About 2 am I awoke and started to drink water as fast as I could. I got woozy again and hit the sack. The wake up call at 5 am was a traumatic event. I eventually made it, but this was not my shining moment.

On another liberty night in San Diego, Al, an older Italian buddy and I were in a local restaurant. While I was flirting with a cute young Mexican waitress, Al notices a medium – built brown - skin guy about 30 years old who sits 3 or 4 seats left of me and Al is at my immediate left. Al notices in a mirror in the back where the food is prepared that the guy has a knife about 8 inches long. In a flash, the guy then moves next to me on my immediate right. Al quickly moves next to the guy and wrestles the knife away before he sticks it into me. The guy takes off like a shot, Al has the knife, my ribs and kidneys are not harmed due to Al's alertness and quick action. The waitress told us that the guy thinks she is his girl friend and of course he is jealous of her talking with anyone else. Al was a good Marine and a very good friend! I struck out trying to make a date with the cute senorita.

Off I went home for Christmas 1945. I was on a thirty-day furlough that would last into January 1946. Here was this twenty-year-old Marine veteran Sergeant with confidence, worldly experience, high self-esteem and a pocket full of money. What a difference from the guy who headed to boot camp in November 1943. We Marines had money because, while on active duty, we were only allowed to collect a very small part of our earnings to prevent the possibility of losing it all in card or dice games – a good policy. Now the money flowed on gals, meals, booze, cabs, shoe shines and dry cleaners. The Marine had to look sharp! Parties, dances, bowling and other activities filled our days.

In Reading, Pennsylvania, about twenty miles from Stowe, a Polish Lodge where we had spent a lot of time before our service duty invited a lot of service men to a big party with free food, booze, and dancing. There was a bevy of girls in attendance. My friend Mike (1st Marine Division – we visited on Okinawa) and I were invited to the big bash. The facility consisted of a bar in one room and a dance floor in another room. The dance floor was surrounded on thee sides by a thirty-inch high railing that separated the dance floor from tables and chairs. As the evening rolled on, the booze started working. Mike and I got into an argument with a couple of sailors over two girls. We each knocked a sailor over the railing and the battle was on! Suddenly everyone was throwing haymakers with sailors, soldiers, and marines crashing all over the place. Calmly, without a bruise, Mike and I headed to the bar and asked the bartender to call the police because a big fight had started in the ballroom. We never found out how many people ended up in jail. I never knew that such uprisings could happen over a couple of girls. We enjoyed the festivities and thanked our hosts for a great return to U.S.A.

On another Saturday night Mike and I hitchhiked to the Polish Club in Reading and had a good time dancing and drinking. On our way back home, we asked to be dropped off at a Greek-owned restaurant. We sat down for a breakfast of: two eggs sunny side up, bacon, hash brown potatoes, wheat toast and coffee. I don't recall the price for the order, but it was probably about one dollar each. We finished the first order and ordered the same meal again. The waitress questioned

Life of a Greatest Generation Survivor

our order but she obliged. After we inhaled the second order, we requested a third. The manager was called to give his approval - he reluctantly agreed. After we gorged ourselves on the third order, we decided that the service they gave us was lousy and that the Greek did not deserve to be paid. We high-tailed it out the back door and started running. In a few minutes, we could hear police cars screaming into the restaurant parking area. We were not caught and we never returned to the Greek's place. Neither Mike nor I were proud of our parts in this terrible episode.

When my thirty-day furlough ended, I headed back to California by train, a 2,700-mile trip, to report for duty on January 15, 1946 at the Goleta Air Station, near Santa Barbara, California. In total I ended up traveling 12,500 miles by train, all at the expense of Uncle Sam. I was lucky, though, all of this free travel by train and ships could have been a "one way ticket." And so this gangly, undernourished kid from Stowe, Pennsylvania went on a journey that included more than 12,500 miles by train and 15,400 miles aboard troop transports with eighty-six days on the Pacific seas from San Diego to New Hebrides to Ulithi Atoll to Okinawa and back to the USA at Terminal Island, California – WOW.

Meanwhile, in Europe, the Nazi – Hun bastards were finally getting their butts kicked by the U.S., British, and Soviet troops. That wacko Adolph Hitler could not face the real world and the state it was in because of his actions. He took the easy way out with a pistol shot to his head. His Thousand-Year Empire came to a bloody end and V-E Day, on May 7, 1945, ended the war in Europe. It was a victory for the good guys, the Allies against the Axis nations. The Japanese surrender came on August 14, 1945 and the more somber V-J Day

John A. Novobilski

came on September 2, 1945 when the surrender documents were signed by the Allied nations and Japanese representatives aboard the Battleship Missouri in Tokyo Bay. People in the U.S.A. celebrated with great joy to hear that World War II had finally come to a winning end!

By now the greatest atrocities that man can inflict on other human beings were being made known worldwide. The Holocaust which was perpetrated by Hitler and his "mad men" on MILLIONS of innocent Jewish, Polish, and Slavic people, by shooting, gassing and burning was the most dreadful act of the civilized world. Less well known is the evidence of brutal and savage treatment of prisoners and enemy combatants by the Japanese. Some of these prisoners were members of own U.S. military and civilian personnel in the Philippines. The Chinese population also suffered greatly. Many of their women were demeaned and used as prostitutes for the Japanese military. The press and other forms of communications were not as vigilant in reporting the Japanese atrocities. The question of why the Japanese leaders were not tried for these acts has never been answered and the Japanese deny the allegations.

On February 15, 1946 I received transfer orders to head back east to the Naval Base in Bainbridge, Maryland. Subsequently, on February 22, 1946 I received my Honorable Discharge papers (a proud time in my young life) and headed home by train. Lots of memories - some good, some bad - flashed through my mind as the train wheels clickety clacked toward Philadelphia, and they continued as the big flakes of snow kept falling and I transferred from train to train on my way home to Pottstown/Stowe. There was no big homecoming event. No one met me at the train station. There was no band music as in the movies. I grabbed a taxi to take me the remaining three or four miles to the house next to the cemetery on Grosstown Road. The family was happy to see me. They were proud of Johnny's service to our country.

As I matured from the experience of my early jobs, college, the Marine Corps and, eventually, my engineering assignments at DWP, I adhered to:

"Ten Principles to Live by Which Have Served Me Well"

>1) Be honest with others and yourself. DO NOT try to be someone else. BE YOURSELF!
>2) Think before you do or say things. Think of what the consequences might be!
>3) Respect adults and persons in authority. However, DO NOT become subservient!
>4) In business or personal dealings, be firm and resolute concerning what is rightfully yours. DO NOT be intimidated by salespeople, lawyers, bullies, or others who try to manipulate, deceive, or cheat you!
>5) When you do something, plan to do the very best you can.
>6) Learn to listen. You will learn more by listening than by talking.
>7) Work harder and smarter. Play fair. Believe in a Higher Being and Yourself.
>8) Be alert and considerate of others around you.
>9) Be courteous. Use the TWO magic words: PLEASE and THANKS.
>10) Integrity and Trust must be earned. NO amount of money can buy these important personal character traits! ~~J.A.N. 1965

Post World War II

One of the first official acts for a returning service man was to sign up for the "52/20 Club" at the State Employment office. This enabled the veterans to receive $20.00 per week for 52 weeks – just come in and pick up the check – no questions asked. Several of my friends really liked this program and used it to the maximum, staying out all hours of the night and sleeping in until noon. After a three or four week break I went back to Doehler Die Casting Co. where I'd worked as a high school student in the precision inspection group. This job was not available, so I was assigned to general inspection. I wanted a more challenging job so I applied for work at the Firestone Tire and Plastics Co., which had been advertising for workers. This was a relatively new plant and the pay was as good as at Doehlers. My job was in the plastics division where plastic sheets and thread was made. Most jobs were "piece work." Certain quotas had to be met to get top pay. After a few months in plastics the workload decreased because of lower demand for the products. I was offered the choice of being laid off or accepting reassignment to tire building. I started building truck tires. It did not take me very long to produce the quota of tires for top pay. I liked the challenge of making my quota much faster than the time allotted. On many occasions I was asked to work two hours into the day shift, from 11 pm to 9 am, so that a Time Study Analyst could measure my work and establish the quota for various size tires. Naturally I slowed down otherwise the quota would be much too high for most of the other workers. If that happened, either quality would suffer or tire builders would never make the quota.

In 1946 we had our first telephone installed! Since I was dating a girl named Angie D. who worked at Doehlers on the day shift, the phone came in handy. I would often take her to work after my shift at Firestone, especially during rain or snowstorms. There was no bus service. She would have had to walk over two miles to work.

In May I decided to take a train trip to Memphis, Tennessee to see my wartime girlfriend Ida Mae. Her letters had continued to arrive even after I'd returned home, but it had been a long, long time since we'd seen each other. When I arrived in Memphis, I called her to arrange for the long-awaited reunion with my Memphis Belle. I found her response strange – she wanted to meet away from her home. We met at a local park and I finally got the word. Tokyo Rose was right again – Ida Mae tells me that she is married to a Navy instructor from NATTC. What a jolt! She had gotten married while I was overseas, but had not stopped writing to me or to my sister Angie. Obviously, I could not understand why she would be so cunning and deceitful. With no reason to hang around in Memphis, I decided to get the next train available to visit with relatives in Chicago and Hazelcrest, Illinois. I visited with Rose (Skobel- Mom's sister) and her husband Stan in Hazelcrest. They welcomed me very warmly. I spent about four days with them. Stan took me out one night to visit some local Polish taverns and we did not get home until around midnight. I crashed into bed. It really felt as if the bed was rotating like a carnival ride; I kept hanging onto the bed frame. It seemed obvious that – hard as I'd tried – I had not drunk Stan and his friends under the table! Aunt Rose felt sorry for me and she chewed Stan out for his poor judgment.

On the train trip from Memphis to Chicago, I had met a cute girl who was attending Northwestern University and we'd agreed to meet at one of the EL transportation stops later that day. Unfortunately, either through my unfamiliarity with the train route or the need for a nap, I missed the stop. When I got back to where we were supposed to meet, about an hour later, she was not there.

Back home, I continued working at Firestone building tires on the 11 pm to 7 am shift. Also, I bought a 1941 Packard Club coupe, the first good car in the family. I was now able to drive Mom to the Polish church on South Street in Pottstown – a six-mile trip by bus. See PICTURE 21.

PICTURE 21 – *John in his 1941 Packard with sisters Annette and Angie along side. Taken in front of house in 1946. I sure would like to have that car today!*

With wheels, visiting the Polish clubs in Reading and the bowling alleys in the area was easy compared to all of the hitchhiking. My girlfriend Angie D. was often at my side as I took her to work or to dances in Pottstown and Reading.

In October 1946 I helped my sister Levina prepare for her wedding to Bernie from Philadelphia. We scoured the countryside to buy live chickens, which would be processed by Levina's friends and parents. This was to be a real Polish Wedding that would go on for at least three days. The Polish church in Pottstown, which had a dance hall in the basement and lots of tables and chairs outside, was an ideal place for the wedding ceremony and reception. A Polka band provided music for dancing and there were plenty of friends, food, and drink. On the Friday prior to the Saturday event, everyone involved gathered for a rehearsal. After the wedding itself, we all worked into the wee hours of Sunday cleaning up the mess. And we still had to try to make it to church services! The party was not over yet, though. The leftover food and booze was moved to our house on Grosstown Road for the Sunday finale. A few days later, Levina and Bernie packed their 1941 Dodge sedan and took off for California. They had planned this move long before the wedding, though they had no prospects for a job or place to live and no relatives nearby.

My good friend Mike got a job at Firestone where he was assigned to work on the Banbury Mixer on the graveyard shift. This was the dirtiest job I had ever seen. It was impossible to keep from getting covered with lampblack powder while feeding the mixer with rubber to give it the distinct shiny black appearance. At the lunch break, 3:30 am, we met to discuss our future at Firestone. When Mike approached me, I did not recognize him. He was covered with lampblack all over except for his eyes. When he talked to me, I flat cracked up laughing! He said that this was it "I quit!" Then he headed for the showers; his days at Firestone were over.

By the way, when we came back home from the war, during 1946 and 1947, Mike and I were invited to several weddings, some local and some in Reading. We usually served as grooms and had the chance to meet new girls – we always had lots of fun!

On February 19, 1947 I decided to join the Marine Corps inactive reserve. It was a non-pay inactive enlistment. This was the FIRST of THREE MAJOR MISTAKES that I made over the course of my life. I will discuss more about this later when the Korean Conflict is in full action. While in the reserves, we would attend informal meetings to keep us up to date on Marine Corps activities as related to the reserve.

Toward the end of summer Mike and I decided to quit our jobs and hitchhike to California to check out colleges out west – the G.I Bill would help us reach our goals. Also, since both of us spent some time in California during our service in the Marines, we liked the balmy weather with beaches and mountains close by. We headed off across the USA with little more than a small duffle bag and the clothes we were wearing. It was very hot through most of the Midwest states, and I think most people who gave us a ride felt sorry for us. We never had any trouble getting a ride since we always looked neat, well groomed, and wore clean clothes. I don't recall exactly how long it took to arrive at Levina and Bernie's little apartment, probably about eight to ten days. During the trip, Mike and I slept under the stars and I do not recall getting caught in any bad storms. Most people were very helpful and talkative. They were interested in our military service. I doubt that it would be so safe to hitchhike across the country these days. Most people won't give rides to strangers because of all the motley-looking creeps, perverts and psychopaths on the loose!

About a month after I got to California, my girlfriend Angie D. from Pottstown made her way out to Los Angeles and called me. It was a real surprise. We got together a couple of times, but the affection kind of faded. I got busy focusing on college and she found a new boyfriend. She eventually got married to a guy from Los Angeles and we had no more contact. Even today, I keep in contact with people back in Pottstown and Stowe through the Pottstown Mercury Newspaper on the Internet. In 2006, Angie D's obituary ran. She died in California and her body was shipped back to Pottstown for burial. She was a sweet girl and I guess my treatment of her was not the greatest. I felt sorry about our break up.

Back then, though, Mike and I were busy requesting catalogues from quite a few colleges. We pored over the school curricula of institutions in Wyoming, Arizona, New Mexico, and California. Mike decided to enroll at the University of New Mexico (UNM) in the school of Pharmacy. He hitchhiked to Albuquerque to enroll at UNM under the G. I. Bill. He got a job washing dishes in a local restaurant, which entitled him to free meals as a desirable bonus. He completed his degree and ended up in San Diego. He visited me at my home in southwest Los Angeles once and that was the last time we communicated. Eventually he moved back east to New Jersey to work as a pharmacist and had little or no contact with his family in the Pottstown area. He never attended any school reunions or had any contact with other school classmates. In 1985, while in Pottstown visiting my sister Annette, I saw Mike's obituary in the local newspaper. He died in New Jersey at age 60. It was a private funeral. Later, I learned that he weighed 450 lbs – two and a half times my weight. The shame about his weight (they had needed a forklift to bury him) was too much for his family to accept.

I decided to attend college in the Los Angeles area and continue to work at various jobs part time. It was too late to enroll at Los Angeles City College (LACC) for the spring semester. However, I could enroll at East Los Angeles City College (ELAJC). A big problem that I had to weigh was the distance and time required to travel to ELAJC. I had no car and would have to use the electric "Red Car Line" which was good and not too costly, but rather slow. The cars were smooth riding on rails and it was easy to study and write while traveling. The distance to ELAJC was about fifteen miles, with a transfer required in downtown Los Angeles. This was compared to a five-mile trip on the Red Car to LACC. Since I was eager to get started, the time and mileage required to go to ELAJC was secondary. Anyway, I figured that I could use the travel time to study. As you recall, I did not have college entrance courses in the Pottstown High School

Vocational Program, so I had to enroll in college preparatory courses such as Algebra, Geometry, Physics and a language class. ELAJC was located in a predominately Spanish/Mexican part of town. I had fun taking Spanish. Actually, the Mexican kids had as much or more difficulty with the class than I did because their grammar was poor with a lot of slang. Fortunately, with good instructors and my strong desire to succeed, my grades were excellent and college was now a viable objective. I will admit it was pretty hard to study alone. All of my classmates lived way across town and I had no wheels! Before the semester was over at ELAJC, I made arrangements to enroll at LACC for the fall 1948 classes in Engineering while also taking classes for a minor in Mathematics.

In the summer of 1948, I decided to go back to Pottstown/Stowe to work and earn some money. This time, instead of hitchhiking back, I answered an ad to share expenses with two other guys (Mel and Sid- Jewish boys) to cover the travel costs incurred by Art, an older Jewish guy, the owner and driver of a 1941 Cadillac Convertible coupe. I don't recall the cost, but one incident near Kearney, Nebraska is still fresh in my mind. As we were rolling east through Nebraska, a tire went flat and we had to stop for repairs. There was a little town close by and Art decided to walk in the direction of some house lights for help. Meanwhile, the three of us put on the spare tire, which was not roadworthy. We would have to wait to get the flat repaired, since it was about 11 pm and garages were closed. When Art got back, it was my turn for a nap so I crashed in the back seat. Art was driving and Mel and Sid were in the front seat. We were back on the road for only a few minutes when we heard the scream of sirens.

Suddenly police cars with flashing lights were coming at us from all directions. Art, sounding panicked, says to us, "Here. You guys take this money," and he starts throwing bills and change at Mel and Sid. We are all completely confused by this and none of us accept any of the money. We stop the car and the police officers surround us. As I poke my head out from the back seat (still somewhat sleepy) an officer points a pistol at my head. "Put your hands up and come out slowly or you will take one in the noggin!" We were all handcuffed, transported to jail, and thrown into a two-man cell. They pulled Art aside for further questioning and we all got locked up for the night. In the morning, they questioned Art again about the robbery of the house where he went after the flat tire. He kept insisting that he was not involved. However, when he was searched during the police stop, they had found a key to the homeowner's car. Now they confronted him with it – this sealed his fate. Art was fined and made to return the loot he had stolen from the house. About 2 or 3 pm the next day, we were on our way again heading east. The three of us gave Art the cold shoulder. You know, on every application for work, licenses, etc., I had to list my jail record. It was a bit embarrassing until I explained the circumstances. Finally, we reach Allentown, Pennsylvania. There I got out of the car to hitchhike the remaining fifty miles home.

Now it was time to get a job to earn some money for the fall semester at LACC. The local bakery hired me to feed the baking ovens. My hours were 5:00 am to 1:00 pm. I don't remember the wages. This was not the greatest job in the middle of summer. I worked on the bakery job for a couple of weeks and then I looked into jobs on the natural gas pipeline being built in the Pottstown area. Well I got the job of "swamper" on the pipe laying crew of a Boom Operator. As I described earlier, this was an outside job and the pay was better than at the bakery. Then it was another trip back to Los Angeles for the fall semester at LACC – September 1948.

At LACC, I enrolled in eighteen units of primarily engineering courses. This was a big load, but I was starting out at age twenty-three and needed to complete about 140 units for my degree. There were some interesting instructors at LACC. In my Civil Engineering Survey course Professor McIntyre was a no-nonsense guy who was very rude to the students. If he saw that you were not paying attention or caught you dozing off, he would throw a blackboard eraser at your head. Students were frightened to enroll in his class and get on his hit list. I had an occasion to challenge comments he made to me. After a heated discussion, we became friends. He invited my wife and me to his date palm ranch in Indio, California. We spent a day there, ate lunch, swam in their in-ground pool, and even took some dates home, too. Another interesting instructor was Newmayer. He taught Physical Education and coached the bowling team. He wanted me to go out for football, but my time was limited and football required a lot of practice. Several years later I learned that his leggy blond daughter hit stardom in the movie world. She changed her name to Julie Newmar. I must say that most of the instructors at LACC were the very best.

While attending LACC, my wardrobe was very skimpy. I used to wear a gray sweatshirt or a dark green nylon jacket over a t-shirt. Sometimes students would stop me and address me as coach. Others would stop me and ask when football practice starts. I used to get a kick out of the questions. While playing basketball at the school gym I ran into the dwarf and actor Billy Barty. He was a real fun guy. In a pick-up basket ball game he would run between an opposing player's legs, which caused everyone to crack – up laughing. He was a real character!

To give me an outlet from all of my studying, I joined a group of young people of Polish descent called the Am – Pol Club, which met on weekends in the Crenshaw District. This is now a predominately black area of town. They gathered for outings at the parks, campgrounds, beaches, and dances at a clubhouse owned and operated by elder Polish men and women. There were no fees to join, just minor expenses to cover food and refreshments at the outings and an admission charge to pay for the dance band. It was a great way to mingle with young ladies and men who had migrated west from all parts of the country. My sister and Bernie usually loaned me their 1941 Dodge to go to the dances. The outings were on Sunday, and I usually bummed a ride until I eventually got a car. I especially enjoyed the "tag" football games in the various parks. I usually played quarterback on teams made up of five or six players. These were very good physical workouts. Generally we would get home about 7 to 8 pm and I would go to work at Firestone to build tires from 12 am to 8 am.

It was at an Am-Pol dance that I met my first wife – Bea. We attended many outings and dances held by the club. We were married in August 1949. She worked for a telephone company as a Service Representative, and I was working as a machine operator at a sprinkler manufacturing plant and attended LACC during the fall and spring semesters. Our combined income was about enough to rent a single-room garage apartment from her family's friend located next to her parent's home on 84th Street in southwest Los Angeles. On July 23, 1950 our first child was born. We named him Frank Carl after his grandfathers.

At LACC on January 26, 1951 I received a Mathematics Minor, Associate in Arts degree.

Due to the Korean Conflict, on February 1, 1951 I was ordered to report for active duty at the Marine Corps Air Station in El Toro, California! This was only eighteen days before the scheduled end of my original February 19, 1947 four-year inactive reserve enlistment. This call to service was unreasonable and unnecessary. I was married with one son and already a veteran of WWII. Yet unmarried guys who had never served and were enlisted in the active (paid) reserves were not being called up! Wait until you learn what kind of duty they offered to me:

1) Work at the Base bowling alleys.
2) Work at the Base golf course.
3) Perform Military Police duty in the local towns near the base.
4) Perform base Fire Station duties as a fireman and, later, in aircraft crash fire fighting and rescue.

What kind of CRAP was this?

John A. Novobilski

I never got a satisfactory answer as to why they needed my service in jobs that could be done by civilians or lower level staff. Still, I had a choice to make. I chose the fire department. I'd never had any experience related to this duty, but it was the only job that would allow me to schedule some college classes. The shift assignments, twenty-four hours on and forty-eight hours off, also reduced my travel expenses. It was a forty to forty-five mile drive one way. After WWII my "gung ho" attitude toward the Marine Corps had been at a level of nine. Thanks to this unfair recall, it dropped to a one or a two! The recall of guys like me resulted in a few on-base Senate hearings – nothing but a lot of rhetoric resulted.

When we first reported for duty, we were assigned to "general duty" status and during this time we took General Classification Tests (GCT). There were four categories of tests:

1) I-138 Reading & Vocabulary.
2) I-145 Arithmetic Computation.
3) I-127 Arithmetic Computation. (Why two different A & C tests?)
4) I-155 Pattern Analysis.

My average score was 144 compared to the general average of 120. Much to my surprise and that of many officers, I had scored one of the highest GCT scores ever. No doubt the two years of college with an A. A. in Mathematics helped.

During the break time, I met Jack, an officer/radar operator who flew on a Grumman F7F-3N Night Fighter and we discussed the test difficulty. A couple of days later, while I was mopping the decks in the BOQ (Base Officers Quarters), Jack pops out of his quarters and says, "what in the hell are you doing here?" With one of the top scores on the GCT, I should not have been swinging a mop. He told me that he would help me get into Officers Candidate School and then an assignment as a Radar Operator on an F7F-3N. See PICTURE 22 of this plane, which had a two-man crew of Pilot and Radar Operator.

PICTURE 22 - *Low Silhouette Front View, of F 7 F – 3 N Grumman Tigercat Night Fighter. Crew: Pilot & Radar Operator.*

In spite of the unfairness of the situation, this Marine carried out his duties with dedication and efficiency. Also, I was now a Staff Sergeant (four stripes), having been promoted on May 21, 1951. So, I requested a transfer to

John A. Novobilski

Officer Candidate School (OCS). My Commanding Officer (CO) informed me of the necessary requirements to qualify for OCS. After a couple of months of taking various dental, physical, mental and technical tests, I only needed a letter of recommendation from the CO. By now, though, we had a new CO. He told me that he could not write a letter of recommendation since he did not know anything about my character. You know what I told him? "You can shove the letter up your ass because I am eligible to get out of this Corps in a couple of months." Did I have the wrong last name? Did I have to be a WASP (White Anglo Saxon Protestant) to be allowed into OCS? Why couldn't he contact my former CO and discuss my character? One other reason that he may have not been too anxious for me to get into OCS was the fact that he was a Warrant Officer and it took him many years to achieve that rank. Why would he want to help me attain a higher rank in much less time than it had taken him? For all he knew, I might have ended up being his CO!

Big Boy, our second son Steve, arrived on December 8, 1952. By now the family had moved to a small house on west 83rd Street, close to Vermont Avenue. It was one of three small houses on a single lot owned by a nice Italian couple —Joe and Frances. We moved into the front house. Joe and his wife Frances lived in the middle house. Their son and his wife lived in the back house. When they moved out, we moved to the back house. Joe maintained the houses very well and we enjoyed having a fine landlord.

On February 18, 1952 I was honorably discharged

– Honorable Discharge No. 2. I often wondered what might have happened if I had completed OCS and became a career Marine Corps officer.

College – Beyond Any Kind of Expectation

Back in the civilian world, I found that we were strapped financially. I still want restitution from the damned politicians for being called back in to do "flunky" jobs! So, it was back to industry. I headed for Firestone – Los Angeles. My application was accepted and after they reviewed my Pottstown record, I was hired at once to build passenger tires on a semi-automatic machine on the graveyard shift – 12 am to 8 am. After a couple of weeks on the job, I applied for a SECOND job at ALCOA (Aluminum Company of America), which was located two or three miles from Firestone. The job at ALCOA, 8 am to 4:30 pm, was in the Ingot section doing time study analyses on various operations. The physical strain on my body building tires and the loss of sleep did not lend itself to doing a good time study job. I quit the ALCOA job after two weeks under advice from my supervisor - a fine man - because I was tardy every day and out of it by 2 pm. The Firestone job provided me with some overtime hours, which increased my paycheck. As I recall, full production of 160 passenger tires for an eight-hour shift gave me about $2.40 per hour or $4,800.00 annually. During this time, I started taking engineering courses at night. Also, the 1936 Plymouth sedan I had purchased for seventy-five dollars was about to fall apart, so we bought a new 1953 Ford, four-door sedan for about $2,000.00 on a monthly payment contract.

Every day I worked as a tire builder it became clearer to me that, if I wanted to get into the engineering profession, the time was NOW. So, I applied to the Firestone engineering department for an entry-level job. They made me an offer that would pay me 30% LESS than my wages as a tire builder. After this disappointment, I applied for a job on a surveyor's crew with the County of Los Angeles. The wages were lower than building tires, but more than the Firestone engineering offer. I soon learned of openings for a mechanical engineering draftsman at the City of Los Angeles Department of Water and Power (DWP). I filed to take the written examination and several weeks later received a notice of the time, date, and location of the written exam. Well, the morning of the exam, I rolled around in bed and snoozed finally waking in a bit of a panic. Though I was afraid it was already too late, I decided to go for it. I made it just in time and completed the exam in about three hours. Two or three weeks later I received a notice of my exam score and a number ranking compared to other candidates. Much to my surprise I was up near the top of the list, making my potential for employment very good. By the way, on all of my applications, under the penalty of perjury, I had to indicate my jail time in Kearney, Nebraska!

Opportunities in the Power Industry

On September 14, 1953 I started my career at DWP. My first assignment was in the Water Department as a mechanical engineering draftsman (MED). This was my first real work in engineering and it was so exciting and interesting to see plans drawn by me made into useful physical projects in the field. I had the opportunity to apply some of my math and physics knowledge to real situations. Also, during this 1953 fall semester I enrolled at UCLA (University of California – Los Angeles) for engineering classes at night. The camaraderie was very good at DWP, and the supervisors were helpful without looking over every move. Even though my pay was slightly less than that for tire building, it was a good place to work in the engineering field and there were many advancement opportunities. The salary at this job was $400.00 per month, equivalent to $4,800.00 per year or about $2.40 per hour.

Our daughter Annemarie was born on December 31, 1953, just in time to make her a tax deduction for the year! Around Memorial Day 1954 we bought a new house (1100 sq. ft., 3 bedrooms, 1 ½ baths) in Panorama City in the San Fernando Valley. Again, the G.I. Bill helped us make this purchase with a thirty-year $12,500 loan at 4.5 % interest. The payment was about $93.00 per month. I joined a carpool to

Life of a Greatest Generation Survivor

reduce travel costs and the need for another car since the distance to work was about twenty miles one-way and bus service was not an option. After a year on the job as MED, I passed the exam for the next level, mechanical engineering assistant (MEA). I was hired as an MEA on September 1, 1954 in the DWP power plant design section right on the same corner where I was accosted for the non salute while on liberty in Los Angeles in July 1944.

My new assignment was in the Piping Design Section. What does one do to design a pipe – just go to Sears and get some plumbing pipe? No, this was the design of high pressure – high temperature pipe with about an eight-inch inside diameter and a wall thickness of about two inches. With insulation the outside diameter was about seventeen inches. And with 1,000°F temperatures and 2,000psi (pounds per square inch) pressure involved, there were a lot of calculations needed to determine the expansion (cold to hot to cold) status and insure that the piping was hung properly. Expansion movements could rip out the hangers and lead to a crashing disaster. The calculations were done according to the Spielvogel principles. There were piping systems that were as much as 150 ft long. Before computers, the calculations on regular calculators took seven to ten days to complete and double checks had to be made to insure the installation integrity. Our group was also responsible for insuring that proper clearance was available for all of the piping, electrical wiring, and equipment as shown on the 15 +/- floor plans. These designs were for the 165 foot tall Valley Steam Electric Generating Plant (VSP) in Sun Valley – San Fernando Valley. My supervisor Carl T. became my mentor later in my DWP career. He taught me the elements of sound managerial practices. Twenty years

John A. Novobilski

later he was promoted to General Manager and Chief Engineer. He held this position for a few years until his heart problems prevented him from further duties.

I kept attending night classes at UCLA for two years, from the Fall Semester 1953 through Fall Semester 1955, completing thirty-four units.

On April 20, 1956 our fourth child, Carl George, named after his grandfather and uncle, was born at the Queen of Angeles hospital. Coincidently, in an adjoining room, a son was born to the wife of my previous boss Carl T. – supervisor in the Piping Design section. We usually met for short chats during our visits to the hospital.

In May 1956 I decided that a "Design Desk Jockey" was not the type of work that was in my future. I requested a transfer to work at VSP as an MEA. The plant was about four miles from my home. I liked the field action and the work was varied, as it related to the operation and maintenance of modern electric generating stations. My boss Herman, Russ the superintendent, and the operating, instrument, chemical and clerical personnel were all very cooperative. There were a couple of ideas that I offered that were adopted and are probably still in use. One was the organization, planning, and scheduling of major inspection and repair of a complete unit shutdown, which could last for two to three months. The outage meant that from 100,000 to 160,000 kilowatts of power was unavailable to the system. This is the equivalent of enough power for 100,000 to 160,000 customers. Itemized schedules were prepared in advance so that the various sections responsible for doing the work could plan their manpower, material, and equipment needs instead of waiting until the last minute or possibly overlooking critical items. This practice came to be required at all plants. It was a money saving process and easily understood by the various working groups involved. A second idea of mine was the use of a plywood pattern that I designed to enable maintenance personnel to prepare heavy, irregular-shaped refractory blocks for the boiler burner replacements. From sixteen to eighteen blocks were placed in a circular pattern close to where the blocks were stored, just as if they were being placed into the burner locations. If they did not fit exactly, they were removed and ground or cut to the right size, and then taken to the job at different levels in the plant. This process eliminated multiple handling under the worst conditions right at the burners. The refractory blocks could be ground or cut to fit during slack time periods rather than during the busy time of the inspection and repair. This was a good, efficient way of using the maintenance crews during off-peak workloads.

In the spring of 1957 I enrolled in night classes at the University of Southern California (USC) because UCLA did not offer some of the engineering classes that were required for my degree. At USC they offered the necessary laboratory courses at night and on Saturdays. By the way, I also enrolled in a Speech class. We bought a slightly used 1957 Chevrolet four-door Station Wagon from a person who was too strapped to make the monthly payments. The wagon was our second vehicle. We used it for the Lodge 3123 outings and our annual treks to the Apache Reservation in the Arizona Mountains.

Working closer to home gave me the opportunity to get

more involved in the White Eagle Lodge 3123 Polish Club and the BSA (Boy Scouts of America). Both of these organizations provided an opportunity for family participation.

The White Eagle Lodge 3123, in the San Fernando Valley, was established in the early 1950's. It is a part of the Polish National Alliance (PNA) of America with headquarters in Chicago. In addition to fraternal activities, the PNA was an insurer of its members and it operated a school of higher education – Alliance College in Pennsylvania. As president of 3123, I and several other active members dedicated our spare time to make the organization family friendly with picnics, beach and park outings, and holiday parties. To supplement our finances we held Polka dances. Our first dance was a tremendous success. It was attended by almost 1,000 enthusiastic dancers. Compared to previous dances held by 3123, we had about five times the number of participants. Actually, there were too many people. We ran out of seating, food, and beverages. The next several dances were not as crowded, but the people (400 to 600) enjoyed each affair much more! Also, to reduce our expenses, we built forty tables that could be easily dismantled, so we no longer had to rent them. To better organize the planning and scheduling process for holding dances, I prepared an outline of all the facets of preparation and execution required, so that officers in the future could use the standard forms to do the job with much less difficulty. These dance format documents were used for future dances and maybe they are still in use. I learned that in a volunteer organization there are two kinds of people - the doers and the talkers. The talkers more often than not will talk a good program and complain about the actions taken by the doers. And they usually dodge doing anything positive. The doers get things done and keep an organization moving in a positive direction. I consider myself to be a doer and am proud of it! In 1962, while we were preparing for a dance at the Carpenters Hall at 7500 Van Nuys Boulevard, I injured my back moving cases of beer from the bar to the floor. I had a lot of pain down my right sciatic nerve. For months afterward, I had to throw my right foot forward in order to walk. My spinal cord was pinched in the lower back area – spinal stenosis. I have suffered with lower back problems for the past forty-five years – I gave my all to the White Eagle Lodge.

I did not have the opportunity to join the scouting movement as a youngster. My parents could not afford the cost of a uniform and the other special items usually required. I wanted my own youngsters to have the chance to be a part of this great American institution (until recently, when the rotten ACLU started to try to dismantle it by their ridiculous lawsuits). I joined another former Marine, Ray, Scoutmaster of Troop 102 in Panorama City, as his Assistant Scoutmaster. See PICTURE 23, 1964 BSA Training Jamboree. Our troop had monthly overnight campouts at beaches and parks, plus local meetings to teach crafts, etc. In our zeal to keep the boys' attention, the activities continued without missing a beat. Our troop became the envy of the area. Membership swelled to the point where we had to cut off additional members. The overnight campouts were the favorite of all activities because the boys could show their stuff as individuals and still work as a team. They probably also liked the freedom of being away from their parents! On June 13, 1958 our fifth child was born and we named her Barbara after her Aunt Barbara.

PICTURE 23 - *Boy Scout Troop 102 –Panorama City, CA. 1964 Jamboree. Mr & Mrs. Breur with Scout Master Ray and Asst. Scout Master John. Troop was very active in Camp Outs and field training in woods and at beaches.*

In the fall of 1958 I requested a transfer to the Scattergood Electric Generating Plant (SSP) to gain experience in the start-up of a newly built facility. This would give me a lot of experience with the latest instrumentation, turbine-generator and boiler systems, and associated seawater systems problems. The drive to the plant was a deterrent since it was about twenty-two miles from home, but whenever possible I tried to carpool to reduce travel expenses. Future assignments and promotions bore out that this was a wise career move. I continued my night and Saturday engineering classes at USC and one of the electives that I enrolled in was Speech. This was a course that this very shy lad needed to tackle, since I had absolutely no confidence when speaking in front of people. Believe me, there were a lot of moments when the sweat poured from my forehead and under my arms. This course made me much more comfortable speaking in public. I learned how to prepare my material and delineate the key points and closing in a more logical manner. For even more practice, I joined the DWP Speakers Club. I made presentations to various local civic organizations to inform them about their Department of Water and Power – our goals, projects, system growth, emergencies, etc.

On February 26, 1960 I was promoted to Mechanical Engineering Associate (MEAc) and assigned to an office back at 4th and Hill Street. Monthly salary for this level started at $721.00 and after three years of satisfactory work it increased to $1,069.00. This was a staff job working directly for the Engineer of Steam Plants (actually, Engineer of Steam Electric Generating Stations). By the end of the 1960 fall semester, I had completed forty-one units at USC. This made me eligible for a Bachelor of Science Degree in Mechanical Engineering, which was conferred on me on June 8, 1961. I shook the guest speaker, President Richard Milhaus Nixon's, hand at the graduation ceremony. DOCUMENT 13 is a tabulation of my Scholastic Record at ELAJC, LACC, UCLA and USC. Thirteen years went by and the suggestions made by a lot of well intentioned folks seemed to infer that without their support I could not have made it! I thanked them. Oh well, they just did not understand the effort it took to complete an engineering degree in the evenings when everyone else was focused on TV shows. In 1961 we scrapped the 1953 Ford and bought a new 1961 Pontiac four-door sedan. Soon after graduation from USC, I passed the State of California Examination for Professional Engineers on my first attempt. This was an all day exam, which required the solution to about a dozen practical engineering problems that might be encountered in the real world. Many candidates had to repeat the exam several times because of its difficulty. On November 20, 1961 I was awarded a license from the California State

Board of Registration for Professional Engineers.

During the 50s and 60s, for the summer vacation, we used to go camping in the White Mountains of Arizona on the Apache Indian Reservation. Also, we visited with the Simpson, Hamilton and Palembas families who lived and worked on the reservation in privately owned buildings on leased Apache lands.

PICTURE 24 - *Camp Out - 600 miles from the Bustling Los Angeles area. Note: The boys' Butch-type haircuts, which they LOVED? They would explore the local streams, lakes, and mountains on their own and try their skills at fishing. A great experience!*

PICTURE 24 shows John, tent, and '57 Chevy wagon in background and cousin Michael, Frank and Steve. This was an idyllic place to unwind and listen to the wind blowing through the pine trees as the kids enjoyed their own adventures in a lake or stream.

Fishing, swimming, and having fun was the order of the day. We capped it off with Spam, beans and onions fried on the camp stove. Or was it onions, beans and Spam? There was the usual campfire at dark to roast marshmallows and some Indian war dances performed by the rowdy ones. The principles we followed when getting ready to move out of our campsite was: 1) Make sure the area looks better than when we settled in. 2) Make certain every last ember of fire has been smothered with water or dirt!

Imagine the cutest kids dressed in their finest clothes with combed hair, and all of them on their best behavior. These were my kids - Frank, Steve, Annemarie, Carl and Barbara - on their way to St. Genevieve's church where Father Ryan was the pastor in charge. This was a time that I will never forget. I will cherish it for the rest of my life. Local families walking into church would look at these nice looking children in awe! Meanwhile, I was considered to be an ogre, "marine sergeant", and other foul names because of the strict and consistent discipline my children were subjected to. However, when it came to campouts with the scout troop, parents liked their kids to be disciplined and taught by the troop scoutmasters – Ray and me. At one point, to cut down expenses, I purchased haircutting equipment and became an amateur home barber. On Saturdays, when "hair cuts will be had" for Frank, Steve, and Carl, there was a lineup of fathers and sons to get a free haircut. In the end, my children became good citizens whereas several of the neighbor kids spent time in jail or used drugs. A few of them even committed suicide or died at an early age.

During this time, I used to do most of the maintenance on our car to try to cut back on spending. Trying to scare up enough money for a six-pack of beer was tough until, Herb, a Lodge member who worked at the local Schlitz brewery, made some available at a bargain price.

John A. Novobilski

While we lived in Panorama City, California my boys got together with neighbors Robert and Larry and proposed building a shack in our backyard. At first, I was a bit reluctant. However, I gave it some thought and the boys agreed to provide me with a plan before they started. Their drawing showing the overall dimensions met with my approval. They scavenged wood and nails and, with some tools borrowed from the neighbors and me, they were in the construction business. As the shack took shape, they decided to include a second floor. Later they started digging a cellar. The project became the talk of the neighborhood. On several occasions there were as many as twelve to fifteen youngsters trying to help. One day I came home from work after the first and second floors were completed and found that the kids were in the process of extending a second floor patio. However, to accomplish this, they'd cut off a large limb of a shade tree that was in the way. I took one look at the butchered tree and told them the project would have to be demolished right then! Of course it was disappointing to them, but they understood that their latest move was not a good one. I often wonder if this shack construction project was the reason all three of my boys - Frank, Steve, and Carl – ended up being such good construction workers, supervisors, and managers. Some of their shack project friends also ended up working in construction. I am sorry we did not take a picture of the shack.

After fourteen years of marriage, Bea wanted out of the miserable life that I provided. Our divorce was final in 1963. She moved out with the two girls. The three boys stayed with me in the Panorama City house. This whole affair was a crushing blow to me and I spent many sleepless nights trying to figure out what I had done wrong. I cannot imagine what the children were going through at this time. All of my efforts focused on my work, doing all of the chores at home (making meals, washing clothes, cleaning the house), and trying whenever possible to help the kids with school work. This was a load, and I depended on neighbors Shirley and Gerry to watch the boys before and after school until I came home from work. Frank, at thirteen, helped a lot with some of the work around the house and with Steve and Carl, which I appreciated very much. As time went by, one by one the boys decided they would rather be with Bea. So, being all by myself, I concentrated more than ever on work and school.

Getting married at my age of twenty-four and Bea's age of twenty was the SECOND MAJOR MISTAKE that I made in my young life. My experience in family relations was poor based on what I was exposed to at home and my service in the Marine Corps did not encourage the sort of sensitivity required for a good relationship. As the saying goes, it takes two to tango, but I will take the major part of the blame for the failed marriage. This was not the way I wanted it to end!

As I moved into managerial positions at work, my attention focused on becoming an effective manager. I studied The Effective Executive by Peter Drucker and tried to follow some of the management principles he covered: Focus on contribution that supplies four basic requirements:

1) Communication
2) Teamwork
3) Self Development and,
4) Development of others.

John A. Novobilski

To focus on contributions is to focus on effectiveness. Executives who ask, "what can I contribute?" are likely to aim at the right things to do and go for achievable goals.

Every organization needs performance in three major areas:
1) It needs direct results
2) Building of values and their reaffirmation and,
3) Building and developing people for tomorrow.

An executive's focus on contribution is by itself a powerful force in developing people. People adjust to the level of demands made on them. The executive that sets his sights on contribution raises the sights and standards of everyone with whom he works! Executives in an organization DO NOT have good human relations because they have a "talent for people." *They have good human relations because they focus on contribution in their own work and in their relationships with others. As a result, their relationships are productive. This is the only valid definition of "good human relations."* Warm feelings, glad handing (politiking) and pleasant words are meaningless.

In decision making, try to establish what is right, NOT necessarily what is acceptable to all. Dissension and disagreement rather than consensus are necessary for good decision-making. Remember, focus on contribution and that RESULTS are the KEYS to contribution! These concepts were very helpful to me in carrying out future managerial assignments.

In July 1964, after passing a written and oral examination, I ranked fourth on the list of eligible candidates for Mechanical Engineer (ME). On May 10, 1965 I was appointed to a new position of Staff ME in charge of seven engineers - two MEAc's and five MEA's - assigned to test and evaluate the efficiency of all four plants' equipment. The potential savings that could be realized by correcting inefficiencies were in the millions of dollars. The MEA's stationed at each of the four plants were also available to provide support to each plant superintendent. Also in 1965, we moved to a brand new modern building on 111 North Hope Street. This was radically different from the old broken-down furniture store building at 4th and Hill Street and very much appreciated by all of us occupants.

Two years later, on May 18, 1967, I was promoted to Engineer of the four Steam Electric Generating Stations. This was at a professional level of success that I never dreamed possible! You know, I thought that if I reached the level of ME it would be a great accomplishment. And so it goes. The DWP had been good to me and, as I promised the Engineer in Charge of power plant design in 1954, I got my engineering degree.

In the job of Engineer of Steam Electric Generating Plants (ESG) I witnessed a few tragic events - the toughest problems to handle and overcome in my power industry career. The first event was a boiler explosion of one 160,000-kilowatt unit (turbine-generator-boiler) at the Scattergood plant. Picture if you can a king sized boiler like a box about thirteen stories high, forty feet wide, and thirty feet deep. The walls are made of high pressure-high temperature steel piping covered by a steel skin with insulation covering the steel skin for safety and to prevent heat losses. This entire structure is attached at the top to massive beams supported by massive steel columns. A boiler of this size is suspended to allow for hot-cold expansion - it would expand almost twelve inches. Because of a problem of volatile gasses being circulated back into the boiler where large gas burners were firing away, the cumulative gasses exploded pushing the walls outward into the horizontal and vertical beams. Fortunately no one was killed, but a few roving operators were blown off their feet and suffered minor injuries. The unit was out of service for about nine months. Repairs totaled about $2 million, not including the cost of using less efficient units to make up for power lost while this unit was out of service. However, investigating the causes of this accident did teach us how to prevent future explosions.

The second tragic event occurred at our newest plant - Haynes Steam Electric Generating Plant (HnSP) - on one of the most efficient units (turbine-generator-boiler) in our system. This was a 320,000-kilowatt unit that suffered a turbine disaster. Consider that this unit operated at the highest pressure of 2,000psi with a main steam temperature of 1,025°F and reheat steam temperature of 1,050°F. That means that the steam was entering the turbine at 1,025 and 1,050°F in two different areas. Somehow, a slug of water entered the turbine. This immediately caused the rotor blades to rip into the stationary housing. The metals fused together and came to a grinding halt. Fortunately, no one was injured, but the unit was out of service for about a year. Again, repairs totaled about $2 million. The cost of less efficient units to provide power while this unit was out of service would add another two or three million dollars to the repair tab. An investigation team determined the cause and, to my knowledge, no further problems of the sort occurred. The teamwork involved in planning, organizing, and coordinating such a project is difficult, but it results in a lot of satisfaction when complete.

24 A – Tatra Mountain Panorama

24 B - Morskie Oko Tatra Mountains

I continued working in this position for a total of five and a half years. There were numerous projects and programs that I initiated while in this section. Working with an outside instrument manufacturer, our operations personnel, and our power design engineers, we designed and built a Training Simulator for Control Operators. See PICTURE 25, Control Operator Simulator.

PICTURE 25- *Steam Electric – Generating Station Simulator. Used for training and re-training Control Operators. Designed and built in 1968.*

This simulator is still being used. Somewhat similar to an Airline Pilot simulator, it is primarily used by seasoned operators as a refresher course about every two years and by newly promoted operators. Using the simulator, the instructor can create scenarios to test an operator's ability to either solve the problem or shutdown the unit.

There were no supervisory training programs related directly to operations, maintenance, or instrument positions. A technician promoted to supervisor was told to do the job "to the best of your ability." Obviously this led to a lack of consistency in supervision. The never- ending change of crews and supervisors that resulted from this lack of a standard caused many difficulties and errors. Eventually, I worked with general supervisors, present supervisors, and experts in related DWP functions (including Civil Service experts) to create a five-day supervisory course designed to cover day-to-day activities. This course enabled both new and experienced supervisors to work more effectively, efficiently and consistently. Similar training programs and manuals were developed and used at every level, from entry level to supervision, in operations, maintenance, and instrumentation. PICTURE 26 shows the Personnel Development Program for Steam Electric Generation. It covers Operators, Maintenance Mechanics, and Instrument Technicians.

To help current supervisors understand the principles of moving up to superintendent, I developed a seven-session course presented in DWP facilities during off hours. Here again, I had current superintendents, Senior Engineers, and experts from other sections in DWP and Civil Service assist in making the presentations. The response was amazing. Many supervisors signed up for this course outside of regular working hours. Eventually, many of these people did move up to superintendent, which is the highest managerial level in the stations.

Management meetings were held about once a month to discuss, analyze, and make recommendations on: personnel relations, cost reductions, operation and maintenance policy, scheduled inspection and repair problems and training programs. We also discussed liaison with other plants and DWP and Civil Service sections that affected the superintendents' activities.

John A. Novobilski

PICTURE 26 - *Shows the Personnel Development Program for the three career paths in the Steam Electric Generating Stations. It shows advancement in Operations, Maintenance, and Instrumentation. It was developed in 1969. In picture – Engineer in Charge Novobilski with Reeve and Dexter.*

After more than five years without a partner, my brother-in-law introduced me to nice lady named Teresa who worked for him in a machine shop. We dated for over a year. Both of us were divorced for five years when we decided to marry in June 1968. Shortly after the marriage we moved to Burbank, which shortened my travel to downtown Los Angeles.

In June 1970, after taking a series of evening classes, I was awarded a Certificate in a Business Management Program for Technical Personnel from UCLA. This was helpful in the administration of higher-level management positions.

My next move was into one of the best jobs that I ever experienced in my DWP career. Having passed the Principal Power

Life of a Greatest Generation Survivor

Engineer examination a few months earlier, on November 6, 1972 I was promoted to Castaic Project Manager. This was a $373,000,000 joint project with DWP (as the design and construction administrator) and the State of California Water Resources (CWR). Water flowing south, over a 1,060-foot drop, in the CWR aqueduct would flow through the Castaic Pumped Storage Plant (CPSP) and generate power. To facilitate the project, Lake Castaic had to be built to store the water that flowed through the turbine generators. The water could continue down to the distribution system with enough water retained to pump back up to the CWR Pyramid Lake located above the CPSP. The pump back of water was done in the low power demand hours of the day, 1:00 am to 5:00 am, by using power from the fossil-fired generating stations. During the peak hours of use by customers, about 3 pm to 7 pm, the water is allowed to flow through the turbine generators to supplement the heavier demand. This process was referred to as "peaking power." Incidentally, this project was built in a brush-covered canyon where years before, as Assistant Scoutmaster, I used to bring our troop for campouts. These were overnight visits a little further up the canyon where the youngsters had streams, hills, and wooded areas to explore.

At the height of construction, there were about 1,200 employees on this project. They included millwrights, electricians, carpenters, steel erectors, machinists, concrete finishers, batch plant operators, ironworkers, equipment operators, hydroelectric plant operators, laborers, engineers, clerical support and others. The final CPSP would consist of six 200,000-kilowatt Turbine generators and one 50,000- kilowatt auxiliary unit for a total of 1,250,000 kilowatts. On October 7, 1973 the first 200,000-kilowatt unit was started and energized to the DWP system. The Start-up Engineer, Dan, coordinated the initial start-up of the unit with me at his side. Later in his career, Dan was promoted to the General Manager and Chief Engineer of DWP. For me, this managerial position allowed me to administer a multitude of activities in the field and office. PICTURE 27 shows two of the seven penstocks as they carry water into the plant turbines. *This job rated Number 1 in my DWP career.*

Unit 1 at Castaic Ready to Roll

PICTURE 27 – *Castaic Pumped Storage Project. Final project has seven pen- stocks, one for the 50,000- kw. Start-up unit and six for the six Main 200,000-kw. units. At top of hill is a large Surge chamber to absorb the shock when units are shut down. DWP was Project Manager.*

After a year as manager of the Castaic Project, I was transferred to the position of Engineer of Generation. This included managerial responsibility for all hydro and fossil fuel generating plants from as far away as Owens Valley to the Los Angeles Basin electric generating stations with a total of about 800 employees. Remember Herman whom I worked for at the Valley Steam Electric Generating Plant

(VSP) in 1956? I hired him to the position of Engineer of Steam Plants at the Basin fossil fuel electric generating stations.

About seven months later, I was reassigned to the position of Engineer of Distribution in charge of all overhead and underground construction and maintenance of the electrical system from the distribution stations to the customers. There were 1.2 million customers within the 454 sqaure miles of the City of Los Angeles. There were about 1,200 employees in the combined overhead and underground comprised of engineers, superintendents, supervisors, linemen, cable splicers, helpers, and clerical staff. Starting in this new position was like being thrown under a bus! I did not have a lot of experience in this area of the power industry. To allow me to get on board, I requested that the two general superintendents and their assistants prepare an organization chart listing the reasons for every employee in their charge and present it to me for discussion within thirty days. This gave them and me a chance to review their organization and evaluate whether they had the proper number of craftsmen to accomplish the goals of each section – overhead and underground. As a result of this review, we concluded that further study with professional assistance was in order. So, in each section we established an in-house study team made up of a supervisor and a craftsman assigned to make field studies with professional consulting team members. Various field jobs were time studied and the resulting crew histograms revealed that:

1) Slack time was excessive.
2) The number of linemen was excessive in most jobs.

3) Jobs requiring overhead and underground work had an excessive number of vehicles on site, and there was overlapping of craftsmen.
4) Vault construction crews were too large with too much slack time.
5) Supervisors were lacking in efficient job planning and scheduling.

After about three months of study and test cases using different crew sizes and staffing, the following recommendations were made and changes implemented:

1) About 25 %, or 100 linemen positions, would be eliminated by attrition at an annual 1980 savings of $2,000,000.
2) Vault construction crews would be reduced by 20 %.
3) A new class of worker would be established at about 12 % higher pay called Electric Distribution Mechanic (EDM), and the class of Lineman and Cable Splicer would be eliminated by attrition.
4) By combining overhead and underground work, five District headquarters were eliminated to provide an additional annual savings of $1,250,000. Qualifying as an EDM would require training in both fields so that, on jobs requiring knowledge of both crafts, the EDM could do the complete job. The efficiency of the Distribution Section combining overhead and underground work improved by about 20-25 % when fully implemented, and the public relations of crews working in the streets was greatly improved.

As in other sections that I was assigned to manage, there was no training for people who were promoted to supervisor. Together with the general superintendents, field superintendents, the study team, representatives from the legal division, human resources section, and other DWP and Civil Service groups, we established a five-day course for existing and new supervisors. This eliminated the previous method where a person promoted to supervisor was given the job and told, "Do the best you know how."

To implement the new class of Electric Distribution Mechanic (EDM), we designed and built a complete training center where entry level Helper to Assistant EDM and EDM's were *trained on actual and live energized lines and equipment.* The success of this program received wide coverage in technical articles and magazines. With the supervisory and craft-level training implemented the section morale was much better.

On April 1, 1976 I was promoted to Assistant Division Head. This position included responsibility for the Division Clerical Section. The Clerical Section only had about 400 employees, and I requested to keep my previous position as Engineer of Distribution with my new job. My higher-level supervisors agreed to the request, however, candidates on the eligible list for Principal Power Engineer did not like my move because it cut out a higher-level promotion for someone. Nevertheless, I did not believe in overstaffing in any discipline. I never received any face–to-face challenges to my move! And now my responsibilities included a staff of about 1,600 people. In all of my jobs as manager, I found that about three to four percent of the people create most of the problems and require the most attention. I took every opportunity to give recognition to the good employees. I tried to learn the first names of these employees during my field visits. They appeared to appreciate these visits. I truly believe that my sincere interest in trying to learn and remember the names of people who worked with me helped my advancement through DWP managerial ranks.

On August 8, 1977 I was appointed to the position of Division Head for the Power Operating and Maintenance Division. WOW, this was a position way above my greatest expectations! (It was probably above my level of competence, too!) Only three more moves up the promotional ladder was the General Manager and Chief Engineer position!!!! The division responsibility included the operation, maintenance, and construction of low voltage power lines, the production at generating stations, transmission from outlying cooperative utilities and DWP owned facilities to distributing stations and delivery overhead and underground to customers. The outlying facilities were located in Delta, Utah; Columbia River Basin in Washington; Palo Verde Nuclear Plant, in Phoenix, Arizona; Owens Valley and Hoover Dam hydro – electric plants. We also planned and scheduled the most efficient dispatch of power from all of these sources and were responsible for customer service calls and repair. Over 3,000 employees were required to provide this service to about 1.2 million customers in the Los Angeles Basin. For a kid with low self-esteem from the "ghetto" of Stowe, Pennsylvania, and who had made it to staff sergeant in the Marine Corps, handling the position of Division Head was the challenge of my managerial life!

As mentioned before, the DWP gave me many opportunities to advance and I did my part by making changes to improve efficiency in the sections for which I was responsible. Time moved on and I eventually began thinking about retirement. One year before my twenty-seventh anniversary with the DWP, I submitted my letter of voluntary retirement to become effective on September 1, 1980. The higher-level supervisors appreciated this because it meant that my replacement could start training for my position. And so, with the accumulated overtime and vacation time that I had earned, it was possible for me to leave the Division Head job on May 31, 1980.

Our plans included a move to Miami, Florida where we had purchased a home in the southwest part of the city. This was close to my wife Teresa's family, relatives, and friends of Cuban descent. As we were packing to make our move to Miami from Burbank I received a couple of calls about doing consulting work in Puerto Rico and the Fiji Islands. We did visit Puerto Rico to discuss the assignment, but it fell through due to a lack of funds. I had no interest in the proposed Fiji hydroelectric power plant project. Living in Miami was a really new experience and I kept busy patching and painting the inside of the house. I had a keen interest in concrete with colors and the use of stamps to make a tile or brick look. I purchased a concrete mixer and took delivery of many ninety-six-pound sacks of cement and tons of sand and gravel for the projects. I installed a sidewalk with a red brick look. Later, I capped the existing walk to the house with a one-inch-thick rust colored brick look. Also, with a helper, we removed the asphalt driveway and replaced it with colored concrete. See PICTURES 28 and 29 showing stamped – colored sidewalks.

In the early nineteen eighties, Miami was a jungle of drug dealers murdering one another and the police were busy trying to slow down street crimes. We were victims of an

PICTURES 28 and 29 - *Picture on the left shows new stamped-red-colored concrete and mixer with wheelbarrow. Picture on right shows rust-colored one-inch thick layer on existing concrete walkway.*

armed robbery by three young males. It was about 1:00 am and Teresa, a lady friend Vicky (visiting from California) and I had just returned from a fashion show in which Teresa's relative had participated. How did these guys know about our return home? They were waiting to pounce on us as soon as we parked the car and the garage door was still open. I have never felt as defenseless as I did when the six foot leader (about 25 years old) of this gang was standing behind my car about seven feet away with his .38 pistol pointed at my head. Teresa and I thought these guys were definitely planning to do something the Japs didn't do – kill me. The other two armed "thugs" went about ripping the necklaces off the girls' neck and demanded wallets and purses. Then the leader, at gunpoint, marched me into the house and slammed me to the floor. Soon the girls were forced into the house and pushed on top of me. I figured it was curtains for me. While one "thug" guarded over us, the other two yanked the drawers from every dresser and cabinet in the house and dumped the contents on the floor. They selected their loot (our property) and placed it onto our pillow cases very quickly (they must have had experience). What irritated me terribly was the fact that as a manager at DWP, I had worked hard to promote the training and advancement of our black employees. We were very upset! However, we have looked back at this traumatic experience and realize that any angry American group is capable of such violent action. So, what do you think - because I bring this traumatic incident up that I am a racisit? I did not do any harm to them and I did not provoke this uncalled for action by them! Would someone please tell me how I should look back and remember this terrible incident?

A Miami detective came out to talk to us about an hour after the attack. He took down all of the information we provided and suggested that we come down to headquarters to try to identify the suspects. He also informed us that, since there were no deaths, the investigation would be given less attention than the string of narcotic related murders. Police manpower was stretched pretty thin. This was a disturbing revelation and we were not very pleased. The stolen money, jewelry, and credit cards were never recovered, and no further information was forthcoming from the Greater City of Miami police department. My trust and faith in the justice system failed again – a very sad result!

In 1982 we decided to buy a second home in Las Vegas. My good Jewish friend Herman invited me to get into golfing. So, at 57, I joined three older guys to make a foursome, and we played three times per week. The par 70 Craig Ranch course in North Las Vegas was a shorter course, but it had enough challenging holes for us old hackers. We had a lot of fun and we golfed in cold, hot (115 °F), and foul weather, which shows that we were addicted to the game. I just loved the challenge and understood that poor scores could only be attributed to the player – blame could not be placed on anything or anyone else! It didn't take me long to become addicted to the game. I now had a better understanding of why some of my co-workers would golf on weekends, holidays, and vacations. My best score at Craig (par 70) was a 73, with 1 birdie, 13 pars, and 4 bogies on December 15, 1995. On April 1, 1996, at age 70, I made a hole-in-one on the Par 3, 175 yard 13th hole. There is a lot of luck involved in making a hole-in-one and many golfers never get one during years of golfing. I had some skill, sure, but I also got lucky.

Also, this move to Las Vegas fit in with my consulting job at the Intermountain Power Plant (IPP) in Delta, Utah with the Intermountain Power Service Corporation (IPSC). IPSC was formed to establish the operating and maintenance organization and my role was that of President and Chief Operations Officer (P/COO) of IPSC under a consulting contract. Delta, Utah is a small town with a population of about 300 people most of whom are farmers. This is Mormon country and practically everyone is a member of the Church of Jesus Christ of Latter Day Saints. The people are friendly and they have a great work ethic, but the circle around their family and friends is very tight. Non-Mormons are not readily welcomed into their daily lives and organizations. As the P/COO of IPSC, I had their co-operation and assistance in carrying out my duties at IPSC mainly because of my position of hiring local people for the various jobs.

Life of a Greatest Generation Survivor

As I noted previously, the Castaic Project Manager position was my favorite, but the position of P/COO was the most challenging and interesting. It required all of the know-how that I could muster. There was NO organization chart. NO employment application. I was the only employee. I reported directly to the five-member IPSC Board of Directors. I shuttled among offices at DWP, Home, Delta, and Salt Lake City, borrowing help to get the organization policies and procedures in action. Cooperation among the various offices was excellent. Within a few months I had to hire a temporary employee, Lloyd, to assist me with the myriad of applications for employment IPSC was receiving from our advertising campaign and referrals. An acknowledgement letter was sent to every applicant. Every month I submitted a report to the Board to inform them of employee staffing, training progress, costs and budget needs, problems requiring resolution and by whom. The first position to fill was a permanent P/COO to (eventually) take my place and help me with the hire of Operations Superintendent, Maintenance Superintendent, Instrument and Controls Supervisor, Training Supervisor, HV – DC (High Voltage – Direct Current) Converter Station Supervisor, Plant Engineer and Clerical Supervisor.

To hire the permanent President and Chief Operations Officer, Lloyd and I reviewed a bundle of applications submitted by candidates from across the country. After an exhaustive analysis of the applications, we concluded that about twelve candidates should be considered. We requested them to appear in Delta for a physical and a written and oral examination at the plant. The written and oral exam took about four hours and was conducted by Herman and me.

John A. Novobilski

I specifically hired Herman to assist me in this important task. From the twelve candidates we selected five who we believed should be recommended to the Board for the final selection. On September 13, 1982 I submitted a report to the Board, which included detailed information about the five candidates. As it turned out, the board selected a local candidate and he was scheduled to start on the job October 25, 1982. The candidate who came in a close second was employed in Indiana as a superintendent.

The following data describe the plant operated and maintained by the Intermountain Power Service Corporation: two 800,000-kilowatt units (for a total of 1,600,000 kilowatts of power) with Babcock & Wilcox coal-fired boilers producing steam at 1005°F and 2,640 psi. The plant operations workforce would require 623 employees. Coal would be shipped by rail from underground Utah mines. The owner of the plant is the Intermountain Power Agency and DWP was the Project Manager. Incidentally, I started the organization of the DWP Project management team in the initial stages. Participants in the energy produced are six California municipalities, twenty-three Utah municipal utilities, six rural electric cooperatives, and one investor-owned utility. The boiler - turbine – generator units are very efficient with a very low heat rate of 7,982 BTU/ KWH.

IPSC workers were hired, as much as possible, from the local towns. About 250 new employees had no power plant experience. They were given operating instructions at the plant by experienced supervisory personnel. A control board simulator designed to simulate problems that could occur on the actual units was used to train control operators and assistant control operators promoted to control operator. All of the training was done in plant classrooms and field situations.

The first unit began commercial operation in June 1986, five years after the start of construction. During construction, the peak number of employees reached 4,500 in June 1985.

To reiterate, the position of President and Chief Operations Officer of IPSC was an once-in-a-lifetime opportunity in this dynamic industry. I was privileged to have it and am grateful to those who appointed me. See DOCUMENTS 14 and 15 for the recognition that was given to me for my contribution to the success of IPSC.

On April 3, 1984, I signed a consulting contract with the DWP to study and make recommendations to improve the overall safety and accident prevention program. A good and capable friend, Distribution Superintendent Joe, who worked with me on the study team regarding distribution field projects, was a party to the contract. Our study took us to all districts and various field operations (maintenance and construction) to determine safety problems. Cooperation with the supervisors and craftsmen was very good except one case, in distribution work in the Owens Valley, where a disgruntled employee would not cooperate. We let him run his mouth and let him know that we were still going complete our assignment without his positive input. He departed the session in a sheepish manner. The study was completed in about four months and an oral and written report was submitted to the General Manager and staff for implementation. A copy of the report is in my file.

John A. Novobilski

Finally, I agreed to one more consulting job related to power plant heat rate improvement for the consultants Picard, Lowe and Garrick Inc. (PLG). This was a study and program development for the Southern California Edison (SCE) and Pacific Gas and Electric (PG&E) fossil-fired electric generating plants. The initial phase of the assignment was carried out in the PLG offices in Newport Beach, California where we worked on a Performance Testing computer program.

Working with a group of younger eager computer kids did not make the task as interesting as I had expected. By now, I was getting weary of the travel, waiting at airports, renting cars, and the lonesome days and evenings in hotels and restaurants. My enthusiasm was pretty low. So, I opted out of the study with PGL after we had meetings with PG&E in San Francisco. The time had come to enjoy retirement and especially golfing, which became my new addiction.

Fall of 1987 rolls around and Teresa and I decide to make a car trip to traverse the "Northern Tier States." This was one of the best, most informative and enjoyable trips we ever made by car. We traveled 6,200 miles through eighteen states using 322 gallons of gasoline for a total cost of $345.00. This averaged out to $1.09 per gallon – rather inexpensive – yes.

Before the start of the trip I wrote letters to friends and relatives in La Crosse, Wisconsin; Pittsburgh and Pottstown, Pennsylvania; Fairview, New Jersey and New Britain, Connecticut to let them know the approximate date we would like to visit with them. This gave them time to leave town before we arrived – Ha, Ha, Ha.

From Las Vegas we drove north through Utah and Idaho into Butte, Montana (a former copper mining town) and on through the nice college town of Bozeman. We were impressed with Billings, Montana, a very well kept city. I thought this would be a nice place to relocate some day from the busy overpopulated city of Las Vegas. However, over the past several years, much to my amazement, I discovered that the summer temperatures in Billings reach into the 100 °F and down below zero in the winter – a wild swing in temperature.

We continued southeast through Sheridan, Wyoming, which was a nice little town. Then it was on through Gillette, Wyoming located in a barren, wide-open prairie with very few shrubs or trees. This WAS NOT my kind of town. The poor people who lived here must have eaten a lot of dust particles over the years because of the winds constantly whistling through town. Further on, into Rapid City, South Dakota, the area became nice again with trees and shrubs reaching all the way up to the famous Black Hills. Here we joined a bus tour to Mount Rushmore, where carvings of four former US Presidents adorn the mountain face. Wild buffalo roam the area around the park, part of the Mount Rushmore visitor viewing, food, and relaxation center. Also close by is the gigantic mountain carving of American Indian, Crazy Horse. This is a project that should be completed soon since it was started about sixty years ago by Polish Sculptor Korczak Ziolkowski and has been carried on by his sons. The project has been financed strictly by donations and revenue from the sale of tours and memorabilia. No government funds have been used for the work on this giant mountain sculpture.

John A. Novobilski

Before the trip started, I envisioned that each town and city would have its own unique character. This proved not to be the case. All of the towns and cities had the same pizza shops, burger joints, drug stores, and hotels. This lack of uniqueness was a huge disappointment.

From Sioux Falls, South Dakota we headed into Minnesota, which changed from raw plains to beautiful rolling farmlands. The highway travel was very good as we crossed the Mississippi River and into La Crosse, Wisconsin. Here we had arranged to meet with Steve, an old school friend, who settled here after World War II and married a local girl named Dorothy. Naturally the discussions went back to the old hometown of Stowe, Pa. Generally, we meet at our Pottstown High School Class of 1943 reunions and it had been only four years since the last one. The following day, Steve and his friend Jim and I went to Sparta, Wisconsin for eighteen holes of golf at a nice city course. Just imagine, two "Honkeys" from Stowe have joined the golfing "elite." It can't be true! The day after that, Steve took us on a tour of La Crosse and we found it rather charming. The next day we were on our way traveling southeast through Illinois and Indiana. Tollbooths – we never saw so many of them as we did driving through Illinois. I suspected that Al Capone was still running the state and his funds came from the tollbooths located about every five miles! Also, the truck traffic through all of the states - Wisconsin, Illinois, Indiana, Ohio, Pennsylvania, New Jersey, New York and Connecticut - was terrible and awfully dangerous!

Every town and city continued to look the same and the fast food business was flourishing.

Life of a Greatest Generation Survivor

Our next stop was in Mars, Pennsylvania where we were going to meet old Marine Corp –Boot Camp buddy Joe and his wife Anna Mae. They lived in a nice part of Pittsburgh in a custom designed home. Here again we did a lot of reminiscing about our platoon members and where they might have spent their careers. After a few days with Joe and Anna Mae, we got on the Pennsylvania Turnpike and headed for Pottstown/Stowe. Here we planned to visit with my sisters Annette and Anna, dining out and taking them to Bridgeport, Pennsylvania to see our cousins Agnes, Alba, and Andy. Also while in town, I stopped in at the Pottstown Library to look back at our West Pottsgrove football and basketball scores and wins and losses during the 1940–41 seasons. Copies of the results are included in DOCUMENTS 4 and 6. We visited with my good friends Don and Everett. Don and I bowled three games at the West End Firehouse where we used to set up pins about forty-five years ago. There were four new alleys and automatic pin setting machines had taken the place of the manual setters we had operated. Whoa, progress abounds. More likely, no one would do the backbreaking manual pin setting job anymore!

The next day we were on our way to Fairview, New Jersey to visit with Aleida (Teresa' sister), her husband Manolo, and their children Carlos and Janet. Traffic was awful. It took us about an hour to find their house. Manolo has been a member and officer of the Lions and the next day he took us, as guests, to the club's "Day in the Country." This was an impressive event with lots of good food, parachutists, antique cars and a very large turn out. We enjoyed the day very much and I fell in love with a beautiful 1932 Packard Convertible Coupe with a genuine "rumble" seat. The event was held on a large tract of land located close to the Connecticut border.

John A. Novobilski

It was on to New Britain, Connecticut to visit with John, an old Marine buddy whom I had not seen for over forty years. John was a retired Assistant Chief of Police for New Britain. While we were talking about our Marine experience from Boot Camp and all through the Pacific campaigns, John blacked out. His wife told us this happened when he got excited. It was the result of a terrible accident he'd had while on patrol on a police motorcycle. A loser criminal tried to run over him during a chase! The effects of the incident cause these blackouts. After a couple of days visiting with John and Helen, we got ready for the trip home.

Notice that we always limited our visits to a maximum of three or four days. We believe that, for the host, guests are like fish left on the kitchen counter. After three or four days, they really STINK!

Off we went back through New York, Pennsylvania, Ohio, Indiana, Illinois, Missouri, Kansas, Colorado, and Utah to Las Vegas, Nevada. It was nice to get back home again!

In June 1993 we planned and purchased airline tickets to visit southern Poland and northern Italy. About that same time I experienced weakness as I performed my normal activities around the house. I was spraying insecticide around the foundation of the house when I felt very weak and unable to continue. I stepped inside and lay on the bed. Teresa said we better go to see a doctor. The doctor, not my heart specialist, started feeding me large doses of procardia. The diagnosis indicated that I had arterial blockages. On June 22, 1993, the day that we were to take our trip to Europe, I was in the Sunrise Hospital in Las Vegas getting an angiogram. The next day I underwent an angioplasty. We had to reschedule the trip for 1994.

The trip to Poland came about because my son Steve, in his many travels, visited Zakopane, Poland and discovered that we still had relatives in the area. Our reason for traveling to Verona, Italy was to visit my daughter Annemarie and her family and in-laws.

We made the trip to Poland and Italy in 1994. Steve joined us since he was the original explorer of my Mom's family Skobel in Zakopane. The town where my Pop grew up, Nowy Targ, was about twenty miles away. To make the trip to Poland, Steve met us in Verona. Along with Annemarie and her daughter Isabella, we drove in a rented van through Austria, Slovakia, and crossed into Poland at Chyzne.

This was indeed a satisfying visit because we would walk the same places where Mom walked, such as to the Old Wooden Church built circa 1850, and on the main street Krupowki. We had relatives on the Skobel side of the family spread from Zakopane to where Mom was born in Maruszyna.

Steve found the Stanley Skobel (Mom's nephew) family – wife Sophie and daughters Eva and Margaret. Margaret is a college graduate who teaches English in a local high school. Also, there was the Wrobel family – husband Stanley and wife Aniela (Mom's niece) with three sons all living in Zakopane. Aniela and Margaret made a genealogy chart of the Skobel family, which was informative and helpful.

We were invited to delicious traditional southern Poland style dinners at Mom's nephew Stanley and Sophie Skobel's home, and to Mom's niece Aniela and Stanley Wrobel's home on the main street Krupowki in Zakopane. We were very grateful to be so welcomed to the country on our first visit. Their warmth and sincere welcome was a great highlight of the trip. My thoughts wandered back to Mom because all of these relatives seemed to display her behavior and smiles. Even though I had a tough time with the Polish language, they helped me through my crude discussions and explanations. Margaret helped to make communication easier for all of us. As it will be shown later, we came back again in the year 2000. See PICTURES 30 and 31 – taken in 1994.

In 1996, at the suggestion of an old Pottstown High School classmate, we moved from Las Vegas to Port Charlotte, Florida. This was a nice laidback place to live and we rented a house in an exclusive gated golf course community.

However, the prices for houses and the association fees were exorbitant, so we bought a nice house in another residential section of town. In our haste to move and avoid additional rent expenses, my friend Bill - a Real Estate salesman - along with the seller pulled a fast one on us with doctored prints of the plan. The square footage was not correct. Bill and his office would not correct the fraudulent sale. We lived in that house for about three years and ended up selling it at a slight loss. I must have spent thousands of dollars battling termites, gophers, red ants, carpenter ants and other types of insects. Also, about ten percent (150) of the floor tiles popped loose and had to be replaced by me! What a nightmare. And it was all thanks to the help of a friend from Pottstown. Like me, he had been in the Marines and built tires at Firestone in Pottstown. You can be sure I told the bastard where to go in the crudest possible language. He had no shame!

PICTURE 30 - *From Right around table:Marian Skobel, Ludwina (Skobel) and Wladyslaw Skalski, Stanley Skobel, John N, and son Steve, Sophie (Dudzik) Skobel & Stanley Wrobel.*

PICTURE 31 - *L to R.: Stanley Wrobel, Teresa (husband Jan)Wrobel, Anna (husband Marian) Skobel, Jan Wrobel, (Teresa's husband), Ludwina (Skobel) Skalski, Marian Skobel, John Novobilski, Sophie (husband Stanley) Skobel, Aniela (Skobel) Wrobel, Steve Novobilski, Stanley Skobel and Wladyslaw Skalski.*

John A. Novobilski

On June 28, 2000 we made another trip to Poland from Port Charlotte, Florida. We met up with Steve, Annemarie, Isabella, her grandmother Rosa, nephew Bernie and his wife Rita at the Krakow Airport. We stayed at the Litwor Hotel located in downtown Zakopane, which had most of the amenities of a four-star hotel. By the way, the money exchange rate was four zloty to one dollar, which was very good for us. In 2007 the exchange rate was two and a half zloty to one dollar. Prior to this trip, Annemarie had visited the area a year earlier and discovered a Nowobilski family through a friend of the Skobel's. Wladyslaw and his wife Teresa (Kurnyta) lived on a rather large farm in a recently built house and had a barn for a horse, cows, sheep and other animals. See PICTURES 32 and 33 of Wladyslaw and Teresa's farm.

PICTURE 32

PICTURES 32 & 33 – *Farm and House of Wladyslaw and Teresa Nowobilski in Bialka Tatrzanska, Poland in 2000. L to R- Rosa Garonzi, Annemarie (N.), with daughter Isabella Garonzi, John N. and Teresa – Wladyslaw was working in his fields, Margaret (Skobel) Gladoch, daughter Sara, Rita and Bernie Rensky jr., Steve Novobilski + Margaret's nephews Maciej and Mateusz Kurek.*

This farm was located in the town of Bialka Tatrzanska. It had a fresh water stream running through the property, which was the source of water for the house. Their son Andrew makes sheepskin coats in his own shop. Daughter Stanislawa is a computer operator and she has a girl and two boys. Daughter Anna is a nurse and she has two girls. We did not have a chance to meet them.

Next it was off to a new Goral adventure. See PICTURES 34 & 35 Dorozka Ride and Picnic with Musicians.

PICTURE 34 - *Dorozka (cart) with musicians. We rode in similar carts to picnic in woods. Margaret and Sara Gladoch in background. Great event!*

John A. Novobilski

PICTURE 35 – *Picnic in the woods with a fire to heat the delicious Polish food. John, Steve & Annemarie with Goral Musicians. A GREAT DAY.*

Margaret (Skobel) Gladoch arranged for several trips and all of us were grateful for her efforts. The Trips: Underground Salt Mines in Wieliczka (north of Krakow); Tatra Museum in Zakopane; 1846 Wooden Church and adjacent cemetery; visit to Czestochowa to view the Black Madonna; a Dorozka Ride (four-seat cart drawn by two horses) to a picnic area with five Goral musicians and cart drivers, all dressed in typical Goral costumes (actual clothes for special events); the Skobel Ice Cream and Pastry Parlor; three Skobel families living on farms, and other local points of interest. Bogus Wrobel, son of Aniela and Stanley, assisted us in our local tours before he left for college He was a very friendly and intelligent young man and we all appreciated his effort.

Margaret and I planned the Novobilski – Skobel Dinner and Dance to be held on Friday July 7, 2000 at the Restaurant STEK. See PICTURES 36, 37, 38, 39, 40 and 41.In addition to reserving a room for our party, we arranged to have four young Goral musicians (Blazek, Pawel, Piotr and a 2nd Pawel) and a young Goral dance couple (Agnes and Derek) entertain us with traditional music, dances and singing.

PICTURE 36 - *Novobilski/Skobel Reunion Dinner July 7,2000 at Restaurant Stek in Zakopane, an opening salute! From left Annemarie (N.) Garonzi, Steve N, Margaret Gladoch John & Teresa N., Bernie Rensky jr. and Ludwina (Skobel) Skalski. NA ZDROWIE ! (GOOD HEALTH!)*

The first order of business was to introduce everyone. Then Margaret and I made some opening remarks to celebrate the event and acknowledge our parents and dear family members who had passed on. After I expressed a few sentences in English, Margaret would address the group with similar words in Polish. We also recognized those people who were responsible for searching out our relatives. Steve Novobilski, Margaret (Skobel) Gladoch and Aniela (Skobel) Wrobel were able to determine the Skobel connections. Annemarie (Novobilski) Garonzi and Margaret Wnuk searched out the Nowobilski family.

PICTURES 37 and 38 - *The Novobilski/Skobel Reunion on July 7, 2000 at Restaurant Stek, Zakopane. Left: Goral Musicians –Blazek, Pawel, Piotr and 2nd Pawel. Right: Wladyslaw and wife Teresa with John Novobilski.*

John A. Novobilski

While we enjoyed our delicious Polish food, the dancers and musicians performed to our pleasure. They really put on a nice program of traditional music and dance. After dinner, we all tried our footwork to the Goral music and I had a chance to dance with Agnes who was light as a feather. My poor knees took a beating.

There were twenty- four people attending this private party. The tables were arranged in a U pattern with the dance floor in the center of the room. Here is the list of the people who were present: John and Teresa Novobilski, Steve Novobilski, Annemarie (Novobilski) Garonzi, Bernard and Rita Rensky, Margaret (Skobel) Gladoch, Rosa Garonzi, Stanley and Aniela Wrobel, Ludwina and son Piotr Skalski, Eva and Andrew Kurek, Sophie Pawelczyk, Kasia Wrobel, Sophie Skobel (Margaret's mother), Teresa and Wladyslaw Nowobilski, Margaret Wnuk and children Sara Gladoch, Isabella Garonzi, Mateusz and Maciej Kurek. Later, Beata and husband Darek Bryniarski with baby Suzanna arrived.

PICTURES 39 and 40 – *Novobilski/Skobel Reunion July 7, 2000 at Restaurant Stek, Zakopane. Left: Dancer Agnes dancing with John and Right: Dancer Derek dancing with Annemarie (N) Garonzi.*

The event was a great success and everyone seemed to be happy to participate in the family gathering – once in a lifetime event.

PICTURE 41 - *Sara, daughter of Margaret (Skobel) Gladoch who represents the future of our Polish customs and traditions is anxious and ready to carry on with a BIG smile! Novobilski and Skobel Reunion adjourned.*

Late in 1999 we moved to Miami to be closer to Teresa's relatives and to get rid of the problems we had maintaining the property in Port Charlotte. We took a slight loss on the sale of the house on Painter Avenue thanks in part to that Pottstown High School friend (?) I mentioned earlier. We sold the Miami house a couple of years later at a good profit and moved back to Las Vegas in 2003. It so happened that the gated community where we bought a house was in a neighborhood where we had looked back in 1992. Also, the house belonged to the wife of my good old friend Herman from DWP days. He passed on in 1993. My THIRD BIG MISTAKE was the second move to Florida back in 1996. This was due to the fact that the Port Charlotte house we bought was hard to maintain and because the Miami relocation left me without golfing friends. Also, there was a lot of traffic congestion and humidity. We do miss the friendly Quinta, Noval, and Suri families and Ana Tarin. Still, we prefer the wide-open spaces and dry weather in the western part of the country!

America is Being Destroyed

We who were part of World War II, the Greatest Generation, which includes those who served in the military and those who sacrificed and worked in industry to meet the military's needs, never imagined that America could or would be destroyed from within! Yet there are signs that the greatest country in the world has suffered great internal damage over the past three generations. These generations can be identified as: The Baby Boomers, Generation X, and The Millennium Generation.

The Baby Boomer Generation, now in their mid-fifties and sixties, are made up of the massive numbers of babies born right after WWII. They grew up during the prosperous years of the 1960s. They were part of the out of control "Hippie" movement led by rich young radicals. Their parents raised them according to the writings of Dr. Benjamin Spock, whose own son committed suicide! If one looks at his method of rearing children, it becomes quite evident that it could only lead to disaster. This is proven by the chaos these radical hippies caused at colleges and universities all across the country. Another example of rules, laws, and traditions being trampled by the hippies occurred at the 1962 Democratic National Convention in Chicago. Under their constant attacks, our society, based on responsible freedoms, the rule of law, religious beliefs, and years of long-standing customs and traditions, was torn apart. Yet these same anti-government youngsters, who were full of idealism, drugs, conflict, and hate, wanted their own rights protected. It goes right back to Spock psychobabble. Spock did not believe in raising a voice or a stick to change a child's behavior. He believed such discipline would cause the young person to lose his or her self-esteem leading to mental illness and anti-social behavior. Related to this was the notion that school grades should never be used to indicate failure. The result? One got by regardless of whether any learning was actually achieved.

During the Lyndon Baines Johnson presidency, he and his Democrat politicians gave away the government and in the process created a new lingo – Entitlements. I voted for this slob Johnson and all of the Democrats before him, but this was my wakeup call to change parties! Somehow it became fashionable to give certain people an entitlement to money, school, or other services even though they did not earn them! *Entitlements should only be given for proven tasks or achievements.* This along with the great financial status of the radical youngsters' parents gave this Baby Boomer generation the more appropriate name of "The ME ME ME Generation." What these malcontents needed was a Great Depression.

Generation X was a smaller one, often called a half-generation that came of age during the boom and bust time of the 1980s. During this time there was company downsizing, disruption in the global economy, and a deep (and well deserved) cynicism toward politicians and the machinations of the political system. This generation, now in their mid-forties to fifties, has doubts about their future due to political and global chaos.

The Millennium Generation is in their mid-twenties to thirties. They are the children of the Generation X and the Baby Boomers. Reared by liberal parents from the hippie movement, they are free wheeling, anti- government (anti-everything!) and tied up in the drug culture. Ethics mean nothing to them. They were exposed to the gentle and generous Mr. Rogers. Everything they do must have a reward attached, and there are no losers! Lifestyle comes before work. To extend their adolescence, they move back in with Mommy and Daddy, since this is more economical and requires little or NO responsibility!

Now let's move into the areas where I believe this country is being destroyed from within. All indications seem to show the destruction of America is being caused by:

1) The Legal System,
2) 535 Politicians in Congress,
3) The Left Wing Media and Shock Jocks,
4) Schools and Universities,
5) Religious Establishments,
6) Wanton Moral Decay and Destruction of Traditions.

The Legal System

For openers, let's look at the death penalty. When a person has been convicted of a capital crime he can sit on death row, at taxpayers expense, and to the aggravation of his victim's family, for more than twenty years. Is this justice? The whole process should be fast-tracked and not be allowed to take more than three to four years. Knowledge that punishment will come without delay should help discourage these aggressors who want to commit such dastardly crimes. It is about fairness to the poor victims. They should be free of the suffering they are put through while they wait and wait for justice to be done. After all, they were not the perpetrators.

About every five years or so, bleeding heart liberals and the ACLU go on a campaign to eliminate the death penalty. They say it is cruel and unusual punishment! What the hell do they call what the criminal does to his poor victim? You know, the same gangs of moralists who want to eliminate the death penalty are front-and-center on approval of stem cell experiments and abortions performed by crushing the skull of unborn fetuses. No one has ever been able to present me with a satisfactory explanation of this twisted way of thinking. Where has good old Common Sense gone?

To the dismay of the general public, our grand and glorious Supreme Court has agreed to review the lethal injection process in death penalty cases. The complaint is that lethal injection is cruel and unusual punishment! Well, how ridiculous is this argument? The high court should have thrown the case out with one comment to the complainants: how did your client treat his victim? Here we see more of the games that defense attorneys and the ACLU play with taxpayers' money. The leaches keep sucking and sucking dollars out of the economy with their frivolous actions. In a recent Nevada study of legal assistance to indigents carried out by a team of judges, it was concluded that more lawyers were needed to carry the caseloads at taxpayers' expense. This will just make it easier to spend more taxpayer money on more frivolous lawsuits, multiple appeals, and eventually a request to increase the number of judges. It seems every new law or procedure just complicates the legal system more and leads to more leniency toward the criminal and less concern for the victim. When was the last time that the legal system came forward with a suggestion to eliminate bad laws and procedures to save the taxpayer some money and improve benefits for victims? Where has good old Common Sense gone?

Another unreasonable aspect of the law is sentencing guidelines. It is difficult to comprehend how someone who is convicted of murder can receive from ten years to life in prison. A reasonable sentence should be a minimum of forty years to life in prison. Lawmakers should readily understand that taking a life is a very serious matter. Over the years, bleeding heart liberals and the ACLU have been working to reduce or eliminate sentences. They have little or no respect for victims. On their agenda, only the criminal deserves the utmost consideration and respect. This is a sad scene in a society that is supposed to be based on the laws of the land. *We are TOO SOFT on criminals. Even while they are incarcerated we treat them like invited guests with TV, books, good food, etc. The common sense and least expensive methods of incarceration, such as those Sheriff Joe Arpaio of Arizona employs, should be used at all prisons in this country of laws.*

Laws today do not protect citizens and investors from the greed of corporate executives and people at higher levels in academia and industry. There are cases where people in the corporate world, such as Bernie Ebbers, Michael Milken, Dennis Kozlowski, Kenneth Lay, Jeffrey Skilling, Andrew

Life of a Greatest Generation Survivor

Fastow and many others, end up with millions of dollars through blatantly illegal methods. They go to trial, are convicted, jailed and fined. The fines are usually only a fraction of what they have acquired through their crimes. It seems to me and most people that ALL of the illegal gains should be returned to the rightful owners. The lawbreakers should be stripped of all the illegal monies and properties in addition to jail time! Where has Common Sense gone?

In Pennsylvania, a Student Loan Agency was found to have spent 2.2 million dollars over five years on giveaways. What a misuse and waste of money. To top it off, they spent 7.5 million dollars on employee bonuses. The organization exists *to provide low-interest student loans,* not for employee gratification!

While on the subject of laws of the land – when are the laws applying to illegal immigration going to be enforced? This country is being overrun by millions of illegal immigrants. What is the difficulty in understanding that they break our laws by entering illegally? The laws are on the books! Have any public servants been kicked off the government dole because they are not doing their job? The lack of enforcement can be attributed to the president, congress and our security department. None of them will step forward and do their jobs – so all of these folks are breaking the law, too! All of the laws in the universe DO NOT mean a damn thing unless they are fairly and consistently enforced.

Okay, so what is the solution to the breakdown of our legal system? Write the laws in simple English. Apply fair and consistent sentences that put victims' interests first and that of the criminal last. Nail down the people responsible for enforcement. Lack of proper enforcement should be punished. And, in death penalty cases, keep the appeals to a time frame of three or four years at most. Hold judges, attorneys, and courts to a timetable with severe penalties for noncompliance. Bring back Common Sense; it is getting late!

Reasons to STOP ACLU are:

1) It uses our tax money to promote anti-USA objectives.
2) It supports child pornography and (NAMBLA) North American Man Boy Love Association.
3) It defends our enemies in court or wherever possible.
4) It opposes National Security such as the Patriot Act.
5) It is anti-Christian and against all Christian celebrations.
6) It advocates open borders and opposes Minute Man-type activities.
7) It is pro-death by supporting abortion, but against the death penalty.
8) It and the United Way are anti-Boy Scouts of America and continue to try to kill the organization because GAYS are EXCLUDED.
9) Its members DO NOT believe in the 2nd Amendment – the right to bear arms.
10) It was founded by long-time Communists and tends to follow Communist principles.

Life of a Greatest Generation Survivor

535 Politicians in Congress

This country has 100 Senators and 435 members of the House of Representatives (they will be referred to here as the 535) to do the business of the people. However, *they are so embroiled in their own self-interests and their lobbyist friends' objectives* that the people be damned! They are paid four to five times as much as the average wage earner they are supposed to represent, and they make sure that laws are passed to make their health plan and retirement benefits the very best. Yet if one were to look at their backgrounds closely most of them would not qualify as good citizens. A young recruit entering the U.S. Marine Corps is taught Core Values. If only each of these 535 politicians understood and performed their duties according to these values the country would be in good hands. Just for the record these Core Values are: 1) Honor. 2) Courage. 3) Commitment.

Most of the 535 either do not understand these values or do not believe they apply to themselves. To get a better perspective on the gang of 535 look at these startling statistics: 1) 117 have been involved in the bankruptcy of at least two businesses. 2) Seventy-one cannot get a credit card due to bad credit. 3) Twenty-nine have been accused of spousal abuse. 4) Seven have been arrested for fraud. 5) Nineteen have been accused of writing bad checks. 6) Three have done time for assault. 7) Fourteen have been arrested on drug-related charges. 8) Eight have been arrested for shoplifting. 9) Twenty-one are currently defendants in lawsuits.

10) Eighty-four have been arrested for drunk driving in the last year. Males have been involved in numerous scandals from homosexual relations with male congressional pages; fleeing from an automobile they drove into a water way and from the rescue of a female companion left to drown; and the acceptance of million dollar bribes from contractors whom they helped obtain lucrative government contracts. There you have a sample of the distinguished (?) men and women who are supposed to be working for we the people. The 535 have lost their Common Sense and they feel NO SHAME over their actions no matter how bad they might be.

Before the DEMOCRATS took over the House and Senate in 2006, the new Speaker of the House of Representatives Nancy Pelosi smeared the Republicans as being leaders in the "culture of corruption." Where did she come up with that handle? She derived it from her own party! Just look at Bill and Hillary Clinton, with Bill leading the "oral sex" movement. Look at people like Barney Frank, Jerry Studds, Ted Kennedy and, more recently, Louisiana Representative William Jefferson who had $90,000 in "cold cash" found in his home freezer by the FBI. He was unaware, he says, as to its origin. Member Democrat Pete Stark was the most recent party star to go into a horrible, dishonest tirade about President Bush that shows how deceitful the Democrats can be to get votes! Common Sense and shame does not exist for the Democrats.

Having been voted into office, what can and should the 535 do to carry out their duties and responsibilities to the people they represent? *Perhaps they can start by not committing the seven Social Sins* as enumerated by Gandhi:

1) Politics without Principle
2) Wealth without Work
3) Commerce without Morality
4) Pleasure without Conscience
5) Education without Character
6) Science without Humanity and,
7) Worship without Sacrifice!

Illegal Immigration

Twenty years ago amnesty was provided for millions of illegal immigrants and that was to solve the problem once and forever. Since that time, the situation has reached critical mass and every effort is being made by the 535 to avoid carrying out the will of the people. They are more interested in what will look good for their respective parties at the next election! Why is it so difficult for the 535 to understand that these illegal immigrants have broken the law? They do not have the rights of U.S. citizens, and they should be deported without further talk and legal mumbo jumbo! A little Common Sense by the 535 would solve many problems – use it!

If the 535 grants amnesty and citizenship to an estimated 20 million ILLEGALS, it means these criminals breaking our laws will be allowed to vote. This will place an even greater financial drain on our government, as they will be sure to vote for more freebie entitlements. Voter fraud will prevail.

John A. Novobilski

To all of the 535 and other bleeding heart liberals: *we who fought and won World War II never in our wildest imagination expected to fight for a country that would open its borders with no questions asked.* Unfortunately, only about 2.5 million of the 16 million of us who served in WWII are still around to see our once great country being destroyed by the 535 and left wing liberals in the media, schools, universities, and religious institutions.

A relative from Poland paid U.S. "shark" immigration lawyers over $10,000 to *immigrate by the immigration laws.* A daughter-in-law is required to travel many miles every two years *at great cost to comply with immigration laws.* Meanwhile, our southern border is open to anyone who wishes to cross over illegally at a cost of ZERO DOLLARS!

Also, I have three sons who have trained to work in the construction industry. Their home base was in the Los Angeles Area until they had to move due to competition with the ILLEGAL IMMIGRANTS willing to work for 30% to 50% of normal wages. My self-employed sons have to spend $500 to $700 each month for health insurance, plus the cost of licenses and bonding. The ILLEGALS just go to emergency rooms for medical attention and pay ZERO DOLLARS. Who picks up their tab? We do!

In 1907 President Theodore Roosevelt wrote the following ideas on immigrants that should apply today:
"In the first place; we should insist that if the immigrant who comes here in good faith becomes an American and assimilates himself to us, he shall be treated on an exact equality with everyone else, for it is an outrage to discriminate

against any such man because of creed, or birthplace, or origin. *But this is predicated upon the person's becoming in every facet an American, and nothing but an American... There can be no divided allegiance here.* Any man who says he is American, but something else also, isn't an American at all. We have room for but one flag, the American flag... *We have room for but one language here, and that is the English language...* and we have room for but one sole loyalty and that is a loyalty to the American people." Hey, 535, don't you see the Common Sense applied to immigration by Teddy Roosevelt?

Yet, we have had politicians like scandalous Ex-Governor Spitzer of New York who tried to do everything he could to give illegal immigrants driver's licenses. He tried this, even though seventy to eighty percent of the state's citizens were against such an illegal action. The state of New York and states across the country are overwhelmingly AGAINST such an irrational and expensive way of handling illegal immigrants. It is extremely difficult to understand how these politicians cannot grasp the fact that these intruders broke our laws. They should not get favored treatment, but instead be penalized by being deported. The costs of illegal immigration to our hospitals, schools, benefits, police, and social services are budget busters. Many studies have been made which analyze these costs, yet the 535 ignore the plain facts.

Energy Plan based on U.S. dependence on foreign oil

Presently *we are dependent on foreign countries for about 60 % of our oil requirements, or 1,870 million barrels per year. This* means we pay about 131 billion dollars per year, at $80 per barrel, to countries that HATE us* and would be happy to destroy everything we stand for. Why can't *the 535* understand our position with respect to our energy needs? Exploration for oil in ANWR (Alaska National Wildlife Refuge) has indicated the presence of vast quantities of oil, yet a majority of the 535 and Environmentalists *(Economy Busters)* block attempts to proceed with drilling. Offshore locations could provide additional supplies of oil. Here again, the 535 and Economy Busters block any steps to take action. It becomes obvious that the Economy Busters are stopping any further exploration, but *they take no responsibility for the economic results.* The day will come when *a flip of the switch will not provide the desired result.* Then the finger pointing will start and the scapegoat power executives will hear all of the charges of malfeasance even though their advice was ignored by the 535!

Senator Harry Reid is the Senate Majority Leader. This is a guy who is in a position way above his competency level and he has the temerity to announce, "the War in Iraq is lost." His rhetoric about electric production is also an aberration. He leads the charge to kill coal-fired electric generating plants. We have an awful lot of coal here in the U.S.A., Harry. Also, Harry thinks geothermal sources will provide sufficient electric power generation. However, neither he nor his advisors have made a realistic evaluation of the number of geothermal sources and the problems associated with the disposal of the subsequent wastewater. Just pump the heavily laden chemicals back into the water table and there will be no problems until years after Harry is gone. Then he and his advisors will not have to take any responsibility for their brilliant actions. If windmill power is the solution, then a realistic study should be made to determine the number of windmill farms needed and their possible effect on the environment. Harry is also in favor of wind generators, but not if installed on the waterfronts near the New England States. Restrictions should apply because of the liberal politicians… call it the Kennedy influence! In the cases of both geothermal and wind power, the total cost per kilowatt-hour must be determined and evaluated compared to other methods. Realistically, I believe we can continue to develop more energy efficient housing and buildings supplemented with solar panels. Also, reduced energy use can be realized if people would decide that they do not have to live in 2,500 to 20,000 square foot houses, like Al Gore, and former presidential hopeful John Edwards. These two drive gas-guzzling vehicles and fly around in private jet planes using 10 to 100 times more energy resources than the people living in average-sized 1,500 to 2,500 square foot homes.

Finally, why aren't utilities allowed to build nuclear electric generating power plants? These plants have excellent safety records on land and on the seas. The Chernobyl, Russia plant, which had the great melt down, was not of the same design as our U.S. plants. The amount of emissions from a nuclear power plant is low compared to fossil fuel-fired plants and the fuel costs are also lower. Yet, environmental groups and the 535 have thwarted the development and refinement of these plants, which supply about 70 % of the Europe's electric generation needs. Common Sense in the politics of the United States of America is LOST! We need a solid energy plan immediately and the 535 geniuses should get busy with the real problems facing this country, not just what gets them points in the next election.

John A. Novobilski

The Iraq War and Future Commitments

Can anyone imagine what would have happened in World War II if we'd had leaders like Harry "the war is lost" Reid in charge instead of Franklin Delano Roosevelt and Winston Churchill? Well, we would be stripped of our freedoms and be used as slaves by Hirohito's or Hitler's underlings. Is victory in Iraq a goal that is not in the best interests of America and those poor souls who are under the yoke of radical terrorists? To give up to a bunch hoodlums is shameful. However, I do realize that *shame is not in the vocabulary of the 535!* If we cannot carry out our commitments to other nations, how do we gain the trust of smaller countries confronted by "bullies" who go on the attack at the drop of a hat?

President Bush made one big mistake with respect to the war in Iraq. He believed he would have the backing of the 535 and the U.S. people as in World War II. But these days we have a bunch of spineless politicians like Reid, Durban, Schumer, Kennedy, Dodd, Pelosi, Murtha, Boxer, Kerry, Clinton, Hagel and many more. Also, he did not bargain on the apathy of our people who do not want to sacrifice anything, especially their tank-like gas-sucking SUV's, video games, I-pods, cell phones and leisure time. Me sacrifice? ME, ME, ME is the name of the game. Most people and the 535 DO NOT believe the Islamic Terrorists mean what they say about their mission to KILL the INFIDELS - the Americans. Before and during World War II everyone at all class levels contributed to helping the war effort. Even prior to service in the military, youngsters like myself were picking up scrap. Others conducted war bond sales. Also, we all lived with the rationing of food, shoes, gasoline, soap, nylon hosiery, and many other items to help the war effort.

Back then, we did not have a bunch of left wing movie personalities such as Sean Penn, Alec Baldwin, Bill Maher, Michael Moore, Robert Redford, Sally Fields, Barbra Streisand, Susan Sarandon, Rosie O'Donnell, George Clooney, and many others talking for the enemy and against our forces. The personalities of our era kept busy making up-beat films that supported our troops and war workers. They helped morale. Some of these folks even enlisted in the various services. There were no colleges or universities or cities that harassed the military the way they did at Yale, Columbia and in the GAY Capital – San Francisco. The reverse was true – support was evident in all walks of U.S. life.

During World War II, the news media did not publish information detrimental to our military. They were careful not to provide information that could aid and abet our enemies. And, if the news media ran an article that accused our military of torturing our enemies because they made them wear pink underwear, or scared them with a barking dog, or had them interviewed by a woman, the paper would quickly lose its circulation. We were living in a tough but good time compared to now, when we have gangs of crack heads, dope pushers, sexual perverts, pedophiles, homosexuals, and criminal gangs roaming the streets. We were free from the constant display of pornography, perversion, and promiscuity being pushed by the movies and radio. There were no organizations like NAMBLA, which promotes man–boy love groups to spread homosexuality and pedophilia. Yes, it was a much better time for our children to grow up and even get some good training in the military.

This country and the freedoms it has are in great danger. 9-11 is a dramatic example of what terrorist Muslim fanatics will do to us! That the 535 and all of the left-wing liberals do not recognize the goal of the Muslims is very difficult for those of us who fought in World War II to understand. We understood the goals of Hitler and Tojo/Hirohito and we did something before it was too late – wake up 535 and all of you Left Wing jerks!

Social Security System

The Social Security System, established seventy years ago, has provided workers with modest benefits in their retirement years quite satisfactorily. However, it was never intended to provide complete financial security to retirees. Today there are fewer persons paying into the system than in the past, even though many, many more will eventually be eligible to collect benefits. Yet, the Democrats in their infinite wisdom have raided the monies that were to be put aside for these future payments. Between runaway entitlement programs and direct raids on Social Security, we now face $43 trillion in unfunded liabilities. This amounts to about $350,000 for every taxpayer. Are the 535 working on any solution to this Congress-inflicted damage? THE ANSWER IS NO! In about ten to twenty years, the 535 who used these funds will be gone and they will have washed their hands of any responsibility. The new 535 will be strapped. What to do? It is time for the 535 to set aside their little kiddy arguments and resolve the problem of a tremendous shortfall in funds that are, by law, due to future retirees. It is frightening as to how few problems the 535 actually resolve. Why do we tolerate their malfeasance? By the way, when the Social Security Act became law, there was to be no income tax on the benefits. That is no longer the case. The Democrats needed more tax money to spend and spend, so benefits are now taxed.

Patriot Act and Profiling

The hysteria of many of the 535 and the ACLU over spying on our enemies and recognizing our adversaries is totally unreasonable and unconscionable. Since when are we supposed to allow our enemies, those who want to kill us infidels, the same rights as our citizens? These constitutional experts of the 535 and the ACLU, and perhaps the Supreme Court, are way off the mark on this issue. They should be more concerned about our rights. Here again, I wonder how we could have won World War II with such radical lawmakers advising President Roosevelt and his Cabinet. Can you imagine giving Hitler, Hirohito, and their gang of killers an edge to defeat us on every battlefield? We had Common Sense during World War II, so why not bring it back when we need it badly?

It so happened that the eighteen terrorists who carried out the 9-11 attack on the U.S. twin towers were men in their twenties of Arab descent. Also, those responsible for other attacks prior to the 9-11 attack were of a similar background. How much more explanation is required as to who are the enemy? These terrorists started the battle and we have to kill all of these bastards or we will be the dead ones. Someday, under the yoke of domination after the overthrow of our government by our enemies, our "rights" advocates will at last understand what was at stake in the War on Terror. Only then it will be TOO LATE.

Income Tax Code Simplification

As you know, there are 90,000 pages of confusion and loopholes in the tax code. Understanding this information requires one to be or to consult with a legal or tax code expert. Whenever I have asked a couple of different IRS representatives what appeared to me to be simple questions, their answers were different. Certainly there must be some keen minds among the 535 who can guide others to get rid of the present tax code and produce a SIMPLER version. The simpler tax code should be one that does not require the help of tax preparers or attorneys. Or is the notion of a simplified tax code hallowed ground where the income tax attorney and preparer lobbyists have the final say. They do not want simplification. They want to make things even more complicated. The 535 should do something – even just to show that all of them are not out of the country or campaigning for the next election.

Left Wing Media and Shock Jocks

The media - print, radio, television and Internet - has a duty to present unbiased and truthful accounts of news. Do they abide by these strict principles? Based on a recent survey of the people who prepare, present, and editorialize the news, eight out of nine are left-leaning democrats or far-left radicals – the tax and spend, more entitlements crowd out to milk the government. When almost 90 % of the news comes from left-leaning news media, including MoveOn.Org, how on earth can we get the real truth? Since the Internet has become very popular, there are more and more stories that cannot be checked for accuracy. From one coast to the other and in the heartland, the liberal and left wing media focuses on the parts of a story that support their own political leanings!

Schools and Universities

Our schools and universities are staffed with teachers and professors who relish spreading the liberal left wing line, whose viewpoints are easily absorbed by young minds. In academia as in the news media, about 80 to 90 % of the tenured intelligentsia spreads liberal propaganda under the guise of free speech. Trying to get one of these educators (?) off the tenured dole is like trying to pull a tooth through an ankle. As long as these purveyors of liberal views set the agenda at universities across the country, there is NO possibility that we can arrive at any place of balance on the serious issues facing our country. Academia has lost all principles of Common Sense. This will not change until the tenure system protecting these people is replaced by a system of advancement by performance.

The most recent tragic trend is Teacher/Child abuse. Here we have schools infiltrated by teachers who have captive youngsters on whom to prey. From 2001 to 2005 there have been over 2,500 cases of Teacher/Child abuse. Who are these teachers? They are children or grandchildren of the "Hippie Generation" who are now teaching our young people. This is a sad commentary and these teachers clearly show the results of the Spock method of raising children.

Religious Establishments

It is absolutely unbelievable that in a profession where the protection and molding of children should be the primary goal there have been such an overwhelming number of cases of pedophilia. This was not an overnight phenomenon, and it indicates a moral decay that has been left unchecked for years. The terrible consequences for the young people involved warrant very stiff penalties. Not enough is done to punish the perpetrators!

In the FLDS (Fundamentalist Church of Latter Day Saints), an offshoot of the Mormon religion, polygamy, sexual abuse, incest, rape, and sodomy have gone on for years. Government agencies have neglected to carry out investigations and trials to stop such unsavory and illegal practices.

Moral Decay and Destruction of Customs and Traditions

What is going on in this country? Since when does having so many rights and the freedom to say whatever we wish mean that it is okay to damage each other and whole communities without any consequences? This country has gone mad with sex, pornography, pedophilia, homosexuality, and transvestite and transgender promotion, cross dressing, gay lifestyle advancement, and using sex to advertise almost everything? It appears that morality has dropped into a cesspool with the result that our children are being destroyed. These are the future leaders of our country.

Our country is steeped in drugs, steroids, and sensuality. Our youngsters are caught up in adoration of movie and sports stars, instant gratification, hedonism, perverted sexual promiscuity, and poor parental models. It is time for some tough love, especially at home. It's time to forget the entire PC (political crap) agenda. It is time to return to the religious foundation our forefathers relied on when they began building this great country. The secular progressives with the ACLU must be stopped! We complain to government when tragedies such as "Katrina" occur, but we have taken God out of our lives, schools, and government offices. How can we then ask why God allows such events to come our way?

When priests are involved in pedophilia and it takes years to correct the situation, it indicates how badly things have gotten out of control. The number of perverts and pedophiles has reached alarming levels to the detriment of society and children in particular. To stop this continuing slide of society into the cesspool requires drastic action. The low-life scumbags, shock jocks, sex advocates, ACLU, and free-love-anything-goes perverts will scream that their freedoms are being trampled. I am sure that our country's founders did not envision that the freedoms they fought for would be so seriously abused. All of the perverts, pedophiles, gay and lesbian, transvestites, shock jocks, pornographers, cross dressers, and sexual deviates should establish a GAY colony of their own *to carry out their twisted unnatural way of life with each other* instead of on our children.

A recent incident of "out of control" actions by the homosexuals occurred in San Francisco when they invaded a Catholic church during Communion dressed in their gay costumes and made a total mockery of this sacred religious event. And they scream and protest for special rights for gays? The nerve of these scumbags is sickening. Did any of the local news media or politicians condemn this activity? NO, the whole damn community is warped. However, they would never try to do anything of the sort to the Muslim religion for fear of retaliation with weapons, protests, and a drive to shut down the city! This kind of behavior must be stopped by whatever means necessary.

And, the very latest in moral decay is to have schools dispense birth control pills to girls as young as eleven without parental permission. This looks like the Hillary Clinton agenda for "It Takes a Village to Raise a Child." A sad commentary! Still, there are millions of people in this country who would like to have her in the White House to desecrate it worse than her husband, Draft-dodging Bill "I did not have sex with that woman" Clinton. Hillary could not run a family or look after the records for the law office where she was employed and she has the audacity to think she can run our country?

So what do we do with the out-of-control breakdown of morality? It is a difficult problem, which keeps getting worse!

Freedom is NOT FREE. We who fought our enemies during World War II did not expect to see such a total breakdown in all phases of our lives. Perhaps a Great Depression will be necessary to get our people off the soft way of life: hours of TV, video games, cell phones, I-pods, watching sports, wild concerts, parent-sponsored underage drinking, body piercing, breast implants for young girls, tattoos, and other free wheeling activities. Or maybe it will take an invasion of our country by the enemy who want to wipe us off the map to wake up the left wing and anti–war apologists.

What is wrong with the politicians and Supreme Court that they stop the process to add amendments to the constitution that would: Establish penalties for desecration of the US flag; Define marriage as a legal act between a man and a woman only; Establish a National I.D. Card to prevent fraud in identification cards and help straighten out the immigration mess; Establish that all US money shall legibly show – "In God we trust" as our founders proclaimed and Establish that the Ten Commandments must be displayed in a visible location at all government offices? Our founders created this great country on these beliefs, so what is wrong with them today?

On June 6, 2007 our esteemed senators had a vote on English as America's official language in an amendment to Immigration Bill, 1348. *Would you believe that 33 SENATORS voted against making ENGLISH America's official language? Thirty DEMOCRATS, Two Independents and one Republican voted against the amendment!* To top it off, four of these senators were Presidential candidates. These people are supposed to represent us. More than 90 % of us agree to have ENGLISH as our Official Language! IN YOUR FACE, FOLKS.

Our leaders need to get serious about illegal immigration to stop this country from losing its sovereignty. We do not need dual citizenship with dual loyalties. We need to get back to the melting pot and not to a salad bowl country. Certainly, we who fought and sacrificed to win World War II never imagined our great country would be destroyed from within by Congress, the Courts, the left wing media and by the apathy of its own citizens. Perhaps it would be an appropriate time for the 535 and the courts to approve, adopt, and ENFORCE something along the lines of the immigration policies used by Australia. Each potential immigrant is evaluated on a case-by-case basis. Finally, our lawmakers should take a hard look at the 2005 speech on immigration given by Colorado Governor Dick Lamm in Washington, DC. He was a Democrat who served as the Governor of Colorado from 1975 to 1987. The following is a "revised version" of the speech, which was last updated on June 16, 2005.

I HAVE A PLAN TO DESTROY AMERICA
by Richard D. Lamm

I have a secret plan to destroy America. If you believe, as many do, that America is too smug, too white bread, too self-satisfied, too rich, let's destroy America. It is not that hard to do. History shows that nations are more fragile than their citizens think. NO NATION in history has survived the ravages of time. Arnold

Life of a Greatest Generation Survivor

Toynbee observed that all great civilizations rise and they all fall, and that "an autopsy of history would show that all great nations commit suicide." Here is my plan:

I) We must first make America a bilingual-bicultural country. History shows, in my opinion, that no nation can survive the tension, conflict, and antagonism of two competing languages and cultures. It is a blessing for an individual to be bilingual; it is a curse for a society to be bilingual. One scholar, Seymour Martin Lipset, put it this way:

"The histories of bilingual and bicultural societies that do not assimilate are histories of turmoil, tension and tragedy. Canada, Belgium, Lebanon and Malaysia all face crises of national existence in which minorities press for autonomy, if not independence. Pakistan and Cyprus have divided. Nigeria suppressed an ethnic rebellion. France faces difficulties with its Basques, Bretons, and Corsicans."

II) I would then invent "multiculturalism" and encourage immigrants to maintain their own culture. I would make it an article of belief that all cultures are equal: that there were no cultural differences that are important. I would declare it an article of faith that the Black and Hispanic dropout rate is only due to prejudice and discrimination by the majority. Every other explanation is out-of-bounds.

III) We can make the United States a "Hispanic Quebec" without much effort. The key is to celebrate diversity rather than unity. As Benjamin Schwarz said in the Atlantic Monthly recently:

"The apparent success of our own multiethnic and multicultural experiment might have been achieved not by tolerance but by hegemony. Without the dominance that once dictated ethnocentrically, and what it meant to be an American, we are left with only tolerance and pluralism to hold us together."

I would encourage all immigrants to keep their own language and culture. I would replace the melting pot metaphor with a salad bowl metaphor. It is important to insure that we have various cultural sub-groups living in America reinforcing their differences rather than Americans, emphasizing their similarities.

IV) Having done all this, I would make our fastest growing demographic group the least educated – I would add a second underclass, unassimilated, undereducated, and antagonistic to our population. I would have this second underclass have a 50 % drop out rate from school.

V) I would then get the big foundations and big business to give these efforts lots of money. I would invest in ethnic identity, and I would establish the cult of victimology. I would get all the minorities to think their lack of success was all the fault of the majority. I would start a grievance industry blaming all minority failure on the majority population.

VI) I would establish dual citizenship and promote divided loyalties. I would "celebrate diversity." "Diversity" is a wonderfully seductive word. It stresses differences rather than commonalities. Diverse people worldwide are mostly engaged in hating each other - that is, when they are not killing each other. A diverse, peaceful, or stable society is against most historical precedent. People undervalue the unity it takes to keep a nation together, and we can take advantage of this myopia. Look at the Ancient Greeks. Dorf's World History tells us:

"The Greeks believed that they belonged to the same race: they possessed a common language and literature; and they worshiped the same Gods. All Greece took part in the Olympic games in honor of Zeus and all Greeks venerated the Shrine of Apollo at Delphi. A common enemy Persia threatened their liberty. Yet, all of these bonds together were not strong enough to overcome two factors... (local patriotism and geographical conditions that nurtured political divisions...)"

If we can put the emphasis on the "pluribus" instead of the "unum," we will Balkanize America as surely as Kosovo.

VII) Then I would place all these subjects off limits – make it taboo to talk about. I would find a word similar to "heretic" in the 16th century that stopped discussion and paralyzed thinking. Words like "racist", "xenophobe" that halts argument and conversation.

Having made America a bilingual-bicultural country, having established multiculturalism, having the large foundations fund the doctrine of "victimology," I would next make it impossible to enforce our immigration laws. I would develop a mantra – "that because immigration has been good for America, it must always be good." I would make every individual immigrant sympatric and ignore the cumulative impact.

VIII) Lastly, I would censor Victor Davis Hanson's book, MEXIFORNIA. This book is dangerous. It exposes my plan to destroy America. So please, please – if you feel that America deserves to be destroyed – please, please – don't buy this book! This guy is on to my plan.
"The smart way to keep people passive and obedient is to strictly limit the spectrum of acceptable opinion, but allow very lively debate within that spectrum." - Noam Chomsky, American linguist and US media and foreign policy critic.

The above Lamm speech gives the 535 something serious to contemplate and act on! However, I believe they are incompetent and will mess up anything they try to resolve.

Closing Remarks

I now close this tribute to my parents for their spirit and the very tough times they had to endure to come to this country. Far removed from the customs and traditions in southern Poland, they made a better life for their children. To them and to all of the dedicated people who fought and sacrificed in World War II to keep us free from the mad dictators, I give my sincere gratitude and thanks! I give special thanks to my wonderful family of three good boys - Frank, Steve and Carl - and two nice daughters – Annemarie and Barbara. They grew up to be responsible citizens and fine examples of independent, ambitious, and focused adults. I salute them!

I must also pay tribute to the U.S. Marine Corps where the training, Core Values, and discipline helped guide me, a green kid, to being a better citizen. With the experience of teamwork and leadership I received through the Marines, I was able to give something more valuable than money back to the community through the Boy Scouts, White Eagle Lodge, and other civic functions and activities. My career in the power industry was also enhanced by my Marine Corps experience and by my focus and pursuit of an engineering degree and management certificate. Also, I am grateful to the people at all levels in the DWP who helped me succeed beyond my greatest expectations! As we Marines say

Life of a Greatest Generation Survivor

to each other, Semper Fi. (Always faithful).

I am grateful to the Los Angeles Department of Water and Power for the opportunities to work with fine people and to advance way beyond my imagination. The retirement years have been special, too!

Someone else who deserves many accolades is Teresa, my wife of more than forty years, who has endeared herself to my five children and me. Over the years, she has provided me with many good suggestions and ideas in my writings, social contacts and projects. And, as my daughter Barbara once said, "Teresa deserves a medal for being able to put up with Dad!"

Finally I must pay tribute to my GREAT KIDS who have become respected and responsible citizens of this country. I am proud of them!

Frank ~   Steve ~   Annemarie ~   Carl ~   Barbara
California   Venezuela   Italy   Arizona   Hawaii

Now tell me ....Are they some kind of GREAT KIDS?...YES
PICTURE 42 ~ "THE KIDS"

Lastly, it has been five years since we moved back to Las Vegas. Teresa and I believe that this is "our kind of town" with 24/7 activities. We enjoy living in our gated community and feel this was a great move into a nice place with fine neighbors. We enjoy summer aquatic exercises with a group of about a dozen neighbors. There is a lot of chatter and jokes! Also, a spa is always available to bubble away those nasty aches and pains. In our compound of 179 homes, the buildings and property are well maintained. About five times a year we celebrate various holidays with dinner parties in our clubhouse, where the meals are made by the "Men's Club" for a minimal cost. The community is located close to the main airport, doctors, casinos, shows, restaurants, and entertainment spots. Traffic is usually not a problem. Although it gets above 100 °F, with the humidity at only five to ten percent the heat is usually not a problem. We enjoy the four seasons with an occasional snowfall in December or January. The neighborhood is quiet without a stream of cars, motorcycles, and trucks buzzing around. And, since this is a 55-and-over community, there are no rowdy adults and kids. This is truly a great place to live and enjoy life to the fullest!

John A. Novobilski 2008

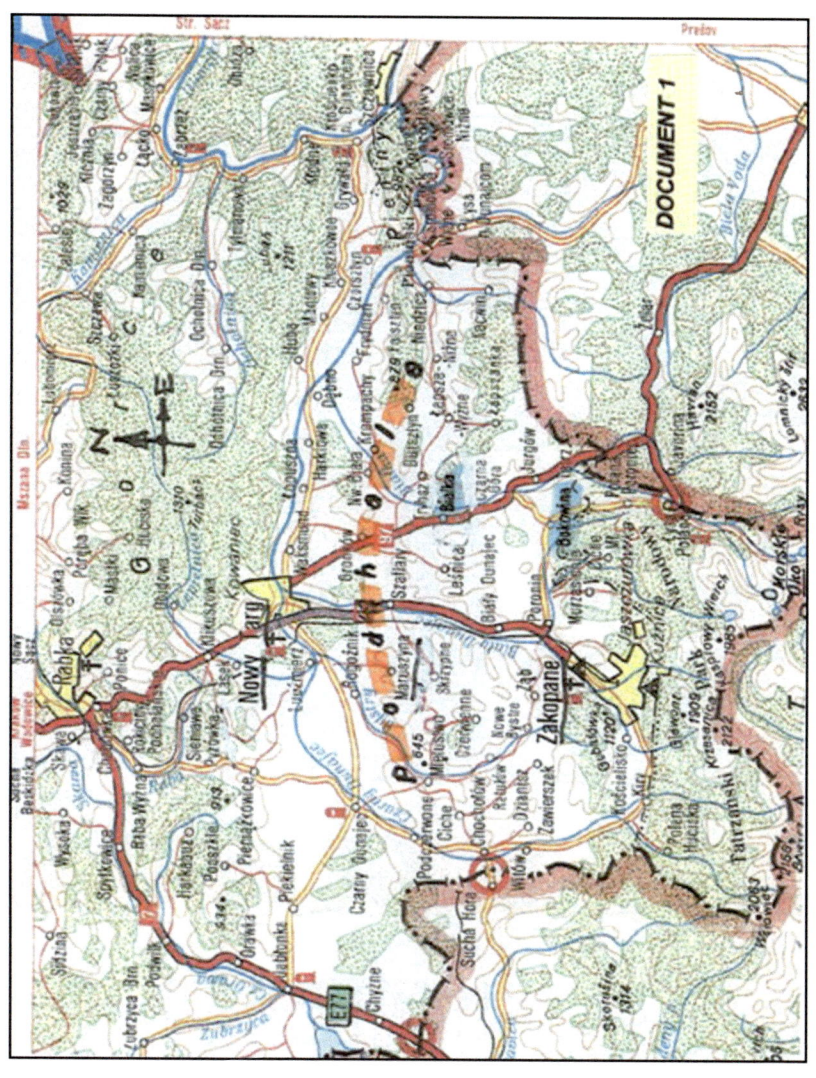

DOCUMENT 1

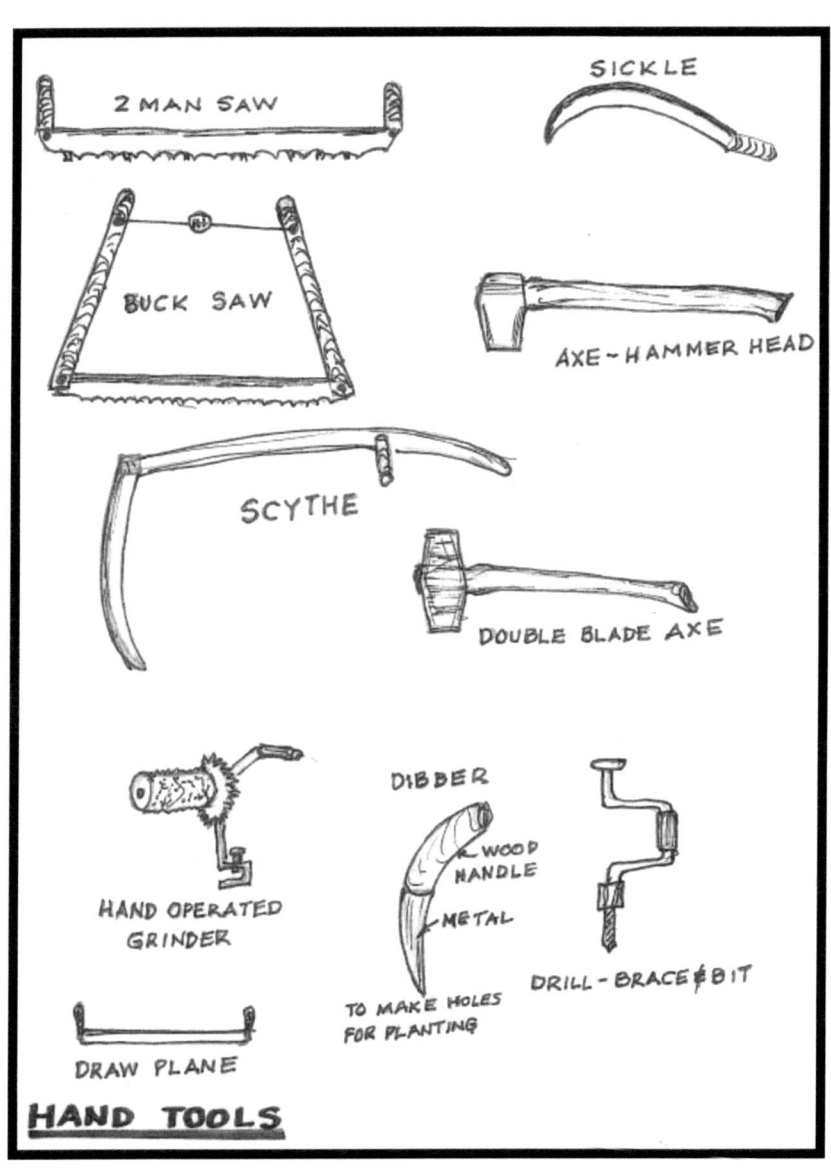

DOCUMENT 2

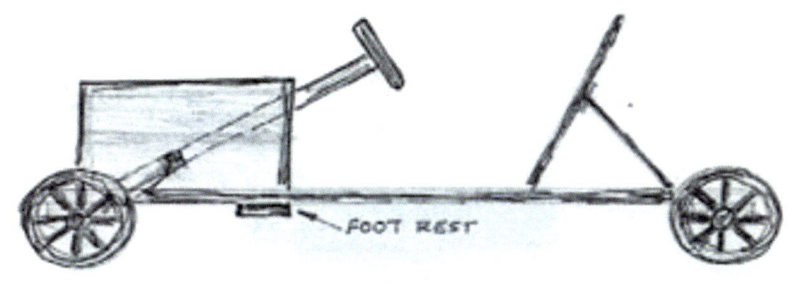

CART 1 – WITH STEERING WHEEL
(To STOP! – DRAG FEET)

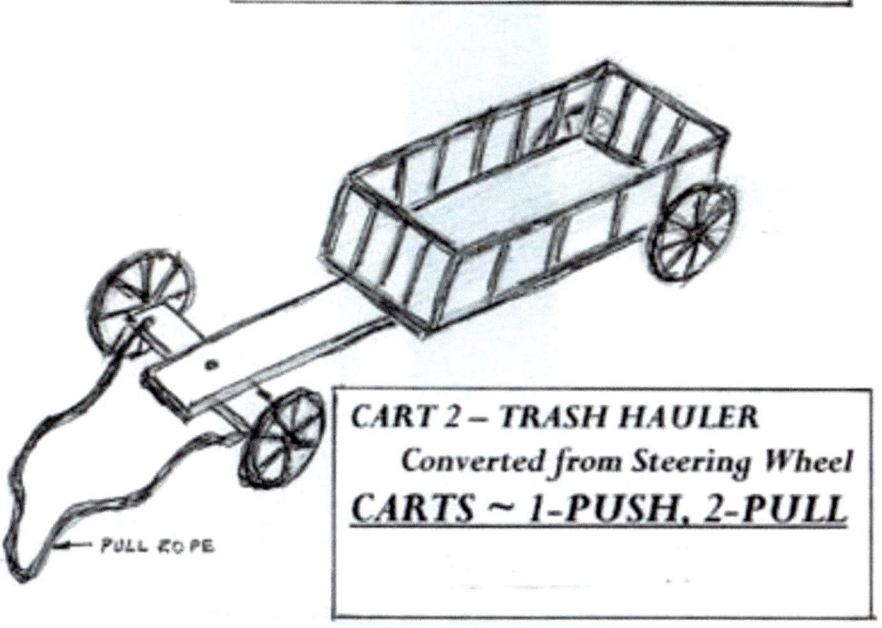

CART 2 – TRASH HAULER
Converted from Steering Wheel
CARTS ~ 1-PUSH, 2-PULL

DOCUMENT 3

John A. Novobilski

FOOTBALL ~ 1940 – 41
WEST POTTSGROVE JUNIOR HIGH EAGLES
STOWE, PENNSYLVANIA

COACH – WINFRED H. BEAN ~
Home Field- Mill Park Race track (2 ½ miles from school)

TEAM MEMBERS:

Don Weaver – LE
Joe Pachik – LT
Al Missimer – LG
Stauffer / Rauenzahn – CTR
Sedleski / Novak – RG
John Novobilski – RT
Frank Ferenz – RE

George Knopp - QB
Bill Breslawski - LH
Bob Plasco - RH
Clarence Gaugler - FB

PLUS; Bob Maimone, Tom Scheidt, Dominic Carlini, James Neri, Len Neri, Pete Zezenski, Mike Strzelecki and John Yarmush.

Student Manager: Doug Weaver

GAMES ~ SCORES: W=Winner

1940 – October

Date	Opponent	Score
7(A)	Boyertown	0......WP......0
12(H)	Darby	0......WP......0
17(A) #	Norco	0......WP......0
26(H)	Upper Merion	18 W...WP......0
Nov. 4 (A)	Spring City	0......WP......0

(A) Away; (H) Home

\# Paul Lucas, Sports Writer for Pottstown Mercury – wrote a story about the lack of offense with Coach Bean and his response was we do not have enough players to conduct a real scrimmage!

Note: September 12, 1940 – New, Buick $1,052., Studebaker $690.

John A. Novobilski – September 1987

DOCUMENT 4

Life of a Greatest Generation Survivor

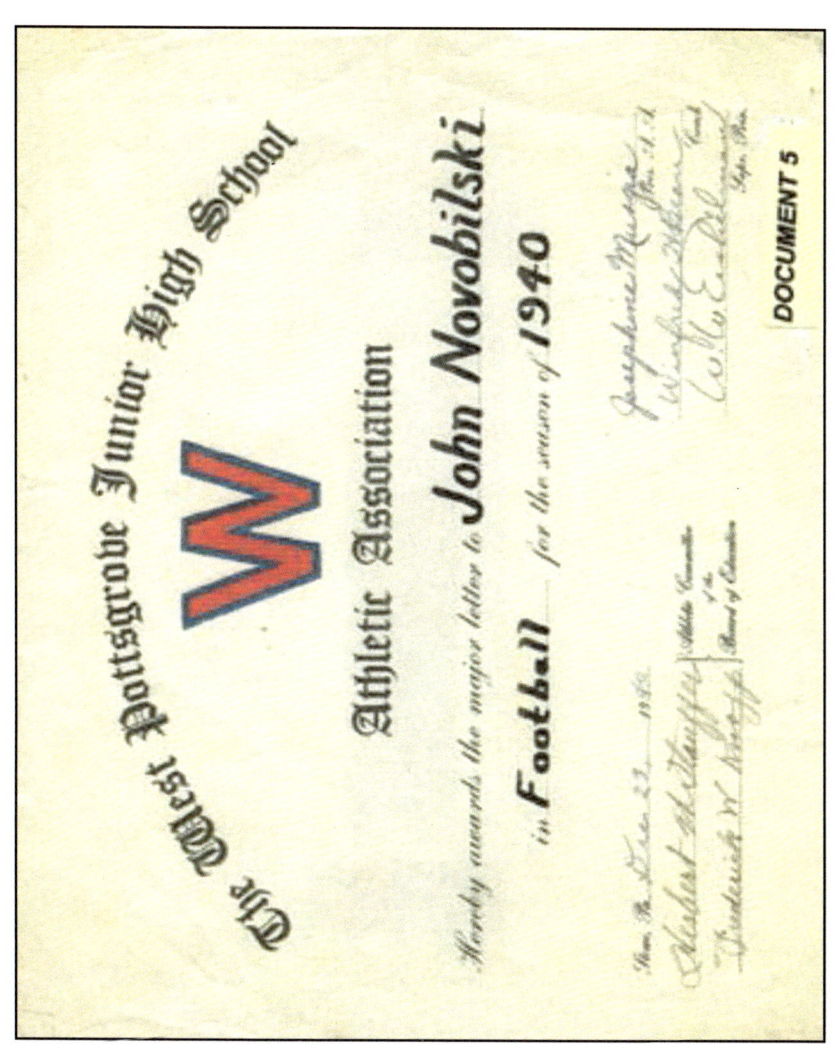

DOCUMENT 5

John A. Novobilski

BASKETBALL ~ 1940-41 ~ BASKETBALL
WEST POTTSGROVE JUNIOR HIGH EAGLES
STOWE, PENNSYLVANIA ~ Coach – Edgar L. Strickland
Home Court Pottstown <u>YWCA</u> (4 ½ miles from school)

<u>Team Members:</u>

Don Weaver........F/C
Frank Ferenz......F
George Knopp......C
Pete Zezenski......G
John Novobilski....G

Other Members: Bob Stauffer- F/G,
Steve Gofus-G, Clarence Gaugler-C,
Lavinia, Maimone + couple others.
Student Manager – Doug Weaver

<u>Game –DATES...OPPONENTS...Score ...WP....NOTES</u>

Date	Opponent	Score	WP	Notes
1941 – Jan. 10	Towamencin	28	39w,	Knopp#, W2, N2
15	East Norriton	14	16w	
17	Rockledge	27w	9	
21	Upper Gwynedd	18	29w,	W12, N4
24	Red Hill	14	32w,	W6, N5
31	Upper Gwynedd	27	32w,	W0, N3
Feb. 7	East Norriton	12	29w,	W7, Nsick
14	Towamencin	10	21w.	W4, N3
21	Rockledge	26w	22	W3, N4~
	WP Lost MONTCO Title			
28	Red Hill	---	---	

<u>Non – League Games:</u>

Date	Opponent	Score	WP	Notes
Jan. 3	Pottstown Jr High..38w......22			W2, N2
28	Warwick	53w.......15		a massacre

Wx= Weaver points and N x= Novobilski points; #Knopp broke his arm in first game and was out for the season.

John A. Novobilski- September 1987

DOCUMENT 6

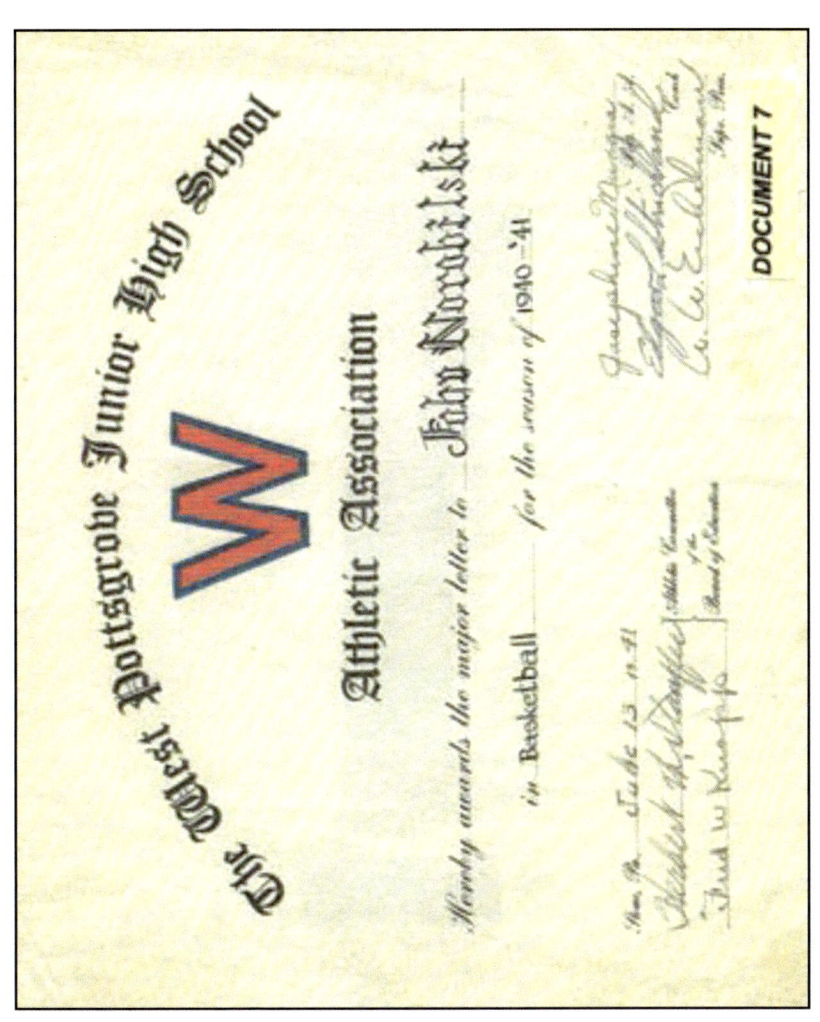

DOCUMENT 7

John A. Novobilski

DOCUMENT 8

Life of a Greatest Generation Survivor

DOCUMENT 8A

John A. Novobilski

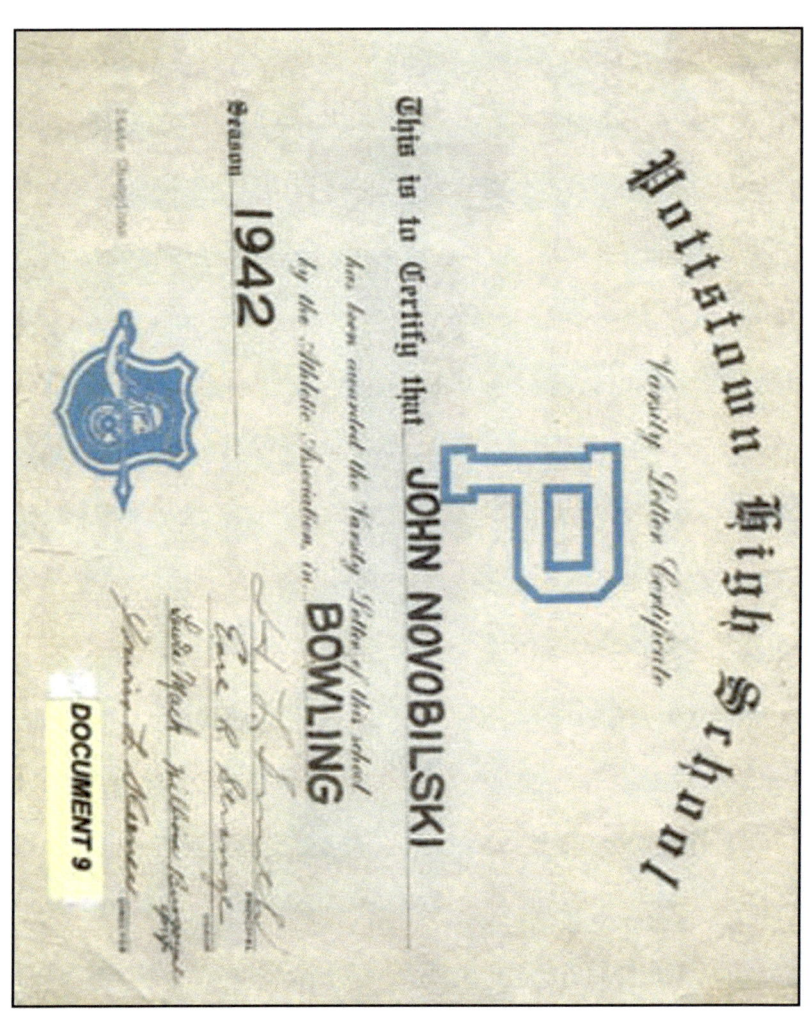

Life of a Greatest Generation Survivor

TRIBUTE to the P.H.S. Class of '43

They survived the 30's "Great Depression",
A struggle which required perseverance and dedication,
With meager funds and tattered clothes,
The goal - a high school diploma - and many obstacles to oppose.
Next it was World War II and they were willing and ready to go,
Abruptly, many changed their goal to fight the axis foe,
While others continued to reach the high school goal.
After that - it was off to war, or, into the work force,
To build our ships, planes, tanks and vital needs to change the course,
Or to the European Theatre to wipe out the Nazi madmen from hell,
Others crossed endless seas to crush the Japanese "banzai" yell.
Some gave the ultimate sacrifice for our families to be free,
And when the war was over it was a victory for all to see,
A victory for freedom - something that makes for great elation.
Back they come - to build a safe and free nation,
With new found energy and the same "guts" and determination.
Do you know who they were ? - the PHS Class of '43,
Pottstown High School youngsters back home from across the seas,
They came back to be known as part of the "Greatest Generation",
The pride of a FREE PEOPLE and a GREAT NATION,
And so, this is a well deserved and long overdue tribute,
To the Class of '43 on their 60th Year Reunion celebration.

by John A.(a.k.a. Noble) Novobilski
Member - P.H.S. Class of '43
September 20, 2003

DOCUMENT 9A

John A. Novobilski

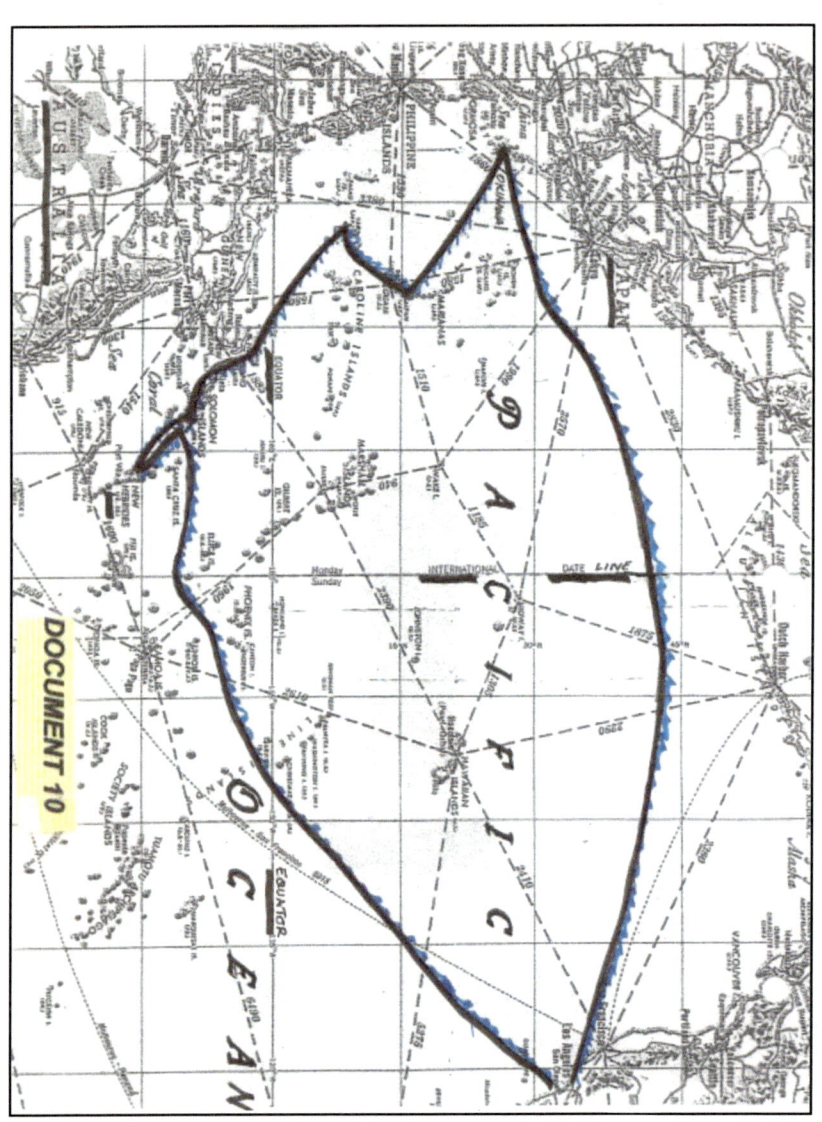

DOCUMENT 10

Life of a Greatest Generation Survivor

DOCUMENT 11

John A. Novobilski

UNITED STATES MARINE CORPS
MARINE TORPEDO BOMBING SQUADRON - 232
C/O FLEET POST OFFICE, SAN FRANCISCO, CALIFORNIA
19 August 1945

From: Commanding Officer.
To: All hands.

Subject: Commendation

Reference: (a) Ltr. CO, TAF to CO, VMTB – 232, Serial: 0093, dtd. 25 May 45

    1. Reference (a) is quoted in part below:

FMP/ res
0093

HEADQUARTERS, TACTICAL AIR FORCE, TENTH ARMY
AND
SECOND MARINE AIRCRAFT WING
25May, 1945

From: Commanding General.
To: Commanding Officer, Marine Torpedo Bombing Squadron – 232
Subject: Commendation.

1. One month ago today Marine Torpedo Bombing Squadron – 232 began flight operations in the Ryukyus area. Prior to 25 April, and since 4 April 1945, the ground echelon has been ashore at Kadena.

2. The flight operations of your squadron have been characterized by aggressiveness, intelligence, courage, resourcefulness and splendid professional skill on the part of your pilots. The execution of close support missions strikes, observations, night heckling and other dangerous and difficult missions have been the admiration of other flight personnel and the subject of much favorable comment and sincere appreciation by the ground forces. Lieutenant F.F. Folino's remarkable exploit in downing a Nip plane at night with rockets is one of the most unique military achievements of the present campaign. His exploit is matched in military effectiveness by mass and individual achievements in support of ground troops.

3. Not only your flight personnel, but your ground echelon too has contributed to the undoubted success of your squadron. The fine results your squadron has achieved are due in no "small part" to the splendid work of your ground personnel in all departments. The assistance they rendered to Marine Aircraft Group – 33 and Marine Night Fighting Squadron – 543, before the arrival of Marine Torpedo Bombing Squadron -232 flight echelon, is especially appreciated.

4. This commendation is addressed without prejudice to and in no way to take place of higher award to which your squadron or yourself is or may later be eligible. I merely desire to let you know, at the end of your first months' operations, how much your work is appreciated and admired by all your comrades in this organization.

"Very well done to all hands in VMTB – 232"

/s/ FRANCIS P. MULCAHY

A. Feldmeier/N
A FELDMEIER

NOTE: Original copy was heavily smeared and difficult to read – this has been re-typed for clarity.

DOCUMENT 12

Life of a Greatest Generation Survivor

```
                        SCHOLASTIC RECORD - John A. Novobilski
         School: East L.A. Jr. College           School: UCLA - Day
                 5357 E. Brooklyn Ave.
                 E.Los Angeles, Calif.     **                                              **
Course                                   Grade   Course                                              Grade
 No.    Subject              Units Grade  Pts.    No.    Subject                    Units Grade   Pts.
        Spring 1948                                      Spring 7-53
  -     Phys. Ed.             0.5   A    1.5      15B    Engr.(Elem.Mech.)            3     B      6
  8     Physics                4    B     8
 50     Math.(Algebra)         5    A    15              UCLA Extension (Night)
 63     Math.(Plane Geom.)     5    A    15              Fall 1953
  1     Spanish                4    B     8      105A   Ht.Tr. & Thermo              3     C      3
                                                 110A   Adv.Engr.Math(Vect.)         2     B      4
             L.A. City College                   110B   Adv.Engr.Math(Diff. eq.)     2     C      2
             855 No. Vermont Ave.                       Spring 1954
             Fall-Spring 1948-49                 105B   Ht.Tr. & Thermo              3     C      3
  1     Math. (Algebra)        5    B    10      103A   Fluid Mech.                  3     B      6
 12     Engr. (Dwg.)           2    B     4      108B   Str. of Mat.                 2     B      4
 67     Math. (Slide rule)     1    A     3              Fall 1954
  3     Chem. (Intro.)         4    B     8      102B   Engr. Dynamics               3     C      3
 21     Physics (Gen'l.)       4    B     8      105A   Mach. Design                 4     B      8
  1     Phys. Ed.             0.5   A    1.5              Spring 1955
 21     Math.(Coll.Alg.)       3    C     3      100A   Circuit Anal.                3     C      3
  1     Chem.(Quan.)           5    D     2      195L   Air Cond. Princ.             3     D      0
  1     Civ.Engr.(Survey)      3    B     6      120    Princ. Engr. Econ.           3     C      3
  1     English                3    B     6              Fall 1955
  3     Math.(Trig.)           3    A     9      100B   Elec. Mach.                  3     C      3
             Fall 1949
 10     History                2    C     2              USC (Night)
  7     Math. Anal.            5    B    10              Spring 1957
 10     Pol. Sci.              2    B     6      320    G.E. (Tech. Reports)         2     B      4
  2     Chem. (Qual.)          5    B    10      313    M.E. (Ht. Power)             3     B      6
  1     Physics (Mech.)        4    B     8              Fall 1957
  1     Phys. Ed.             0.5   A    1.5     326L   G.E. (Met. Lab.)             1     A      3
             Spring 1950                         452    G.E. (Contracts in Engr.)    3     C      3
  7     Chem. (Organic)        3    C     3      310L   G.E. (Fluid Mech. Lab.)      1     B      2
 21     M.E.(Metallurg.)       3    B     6              Spring 1958
  2     English                3    D     6      333L   M.E. (Metallog.)             3     B      6
  8     Math.(Calc-1st)        5    B    10      276L   M.E. (Mechanisms)            2     C      2
 10     Health Ed.             2    A     6      300    Econ. (Fund.)                3     B      6
  7     Phys.(Ht.& Fluids)     3    A     9              Fall 1958
  1     Phys. Ed.             0.5   B     1      100A   Speech (Pub. Spkg.)          3     B      6
             Fall 1950                           342L   M.E. Lab.                    2     A      6
 18     G.E.(Elem.Mech.)       3    C     3      431    M.E. (Ht. Transf.)           3     B      6
 20     M.E.(Mat.Process)      3    B     6              Spring 1959
 11     Math.(Calc-2nd)        3    A     9      404    M.E. (Dyn. of Mech.)         3     C      6
 21     Psychology             3    B     6              Fall 1959
  3     Phys.(Elec.& Mag.)     3    B     6      481    M.E. (Ht. & Vent.)           3     A      9
             Spring 1-52 (Night)                 490A   M.E. (Spec. Prob.)           1     C      1
 12     Math.(Calc-3rd)        3    C     3              Spring 1960
             Fall 9-52                           305    Engl. (Vocab. Bldg.)         1     C      1
  1     G.E.(Descr.Geom.)      3    B     6      142L   Phys. (Lt. & Sound)          2     C      2
                                                          Fall 1960
                                                 472    M.E. (Stm. Plant Des.)       3     A      9
  **-Grade Points Based on: A = 3                325L   E.E. (Mach. Lab.)            1     B      2
                            B = 2                329L   E.E. (Electron Lab.)         1     B      2
                            C = 1                        Graduated 1-61
                            D = 0                       BSME from Univ. of So. Calif.
```

DOCUMENT 13

John A. Novobilski

INTERMOUNTAIN POWER SERVICE CORPORATION

January 5, 1983

Mr. John A. Novobilski
35 Harbor Shores
Key West, Florida 33040

Dear John:

      The Intermountain Power Service Corporation (Service) Board of Directors (Board) at its meeting on December 17, 1982 unanimously adopted the enclosed resolution commending and thanking you for your key assistance in initiating Service's corporate activities.

      You were appointed as Service's first President and Chief Operations Officer because the Board was confident that with your managerial experience and personal traits you would perform, in a professional manner, the variety of activities necessary to get Service started in the right direction. During your term of office, we received from you much more than we expected and thanks to you Service is well on its way.

      We look forward to further contact with you in the future as we seek your input as a consultant on Service's continuing activities.

      Thank you again.

Sincerely,

Raymond C. Burt

RAYMOND C. BURT
Chairman of the Board

Enclosure

cc: Board of Directors
    Joseph C. Fackrell
    James H. Anthony
    S. Gale Chapman

Brush Wellman Road, Delta, Utah / Mailing Address: P.O. Box 864, Delta, Utah 84624 / Telephone: (801) 864-4414

DOCUMENT 14

Life of a Greatest Generation Survivor

RESOLUTION IPSC - 1982-035

WHEREAS, Mr. John A. Novobilski recently completed his term of office as the first President and Chief Operations Officer of Intermountain Power Service Corporation (Service); and

WHEREAS, Mr. Novobilski carried out the responsibilities of his position with skill, dedication, integrity and superior effort; and

WHEREAS, Mr. Novobilski has left an organizational legacy to Service through his work in the development of Service's initial programs and the hiring of key managers; and

WHEREAS, the Board of Directors of Service is grateful for the work done by Mr. Novobilski in helping to organize Service; therefore,

BE IT RESOLVED BY THE BOARD OF DIRECTORS (Board) of Service that Mr. John A. Novobilski, first President and Chief Operations Officer of Service, is hereby commended by the Board for his contributions to and the effort put forth in helping to organize Service.

This Resolution shall be in full force and effect immediately upon its adoption.

Adopted by the Intermountain Power Service Corporation on December 17, 1982.

INTERMOUNTAIN POWER SERVICE CORPORATION

Raymond C. Burt
CHAIRMAN

ATTEST *Arthur S. Buchanan*
SECRETARY

DOCUMENT 15